The Merrill Studies
in
The Sound and the Fury

CHARLES E. MERRILL STUDIES

Under the General Editorship of
Matthew J. Bruccoli and Joseph Katz

The Merrill Studies in The Sound and the Fury

Compiled by

James B. Meriwether
University of South Carolina

Charles E. Merrill Publishing Company
A Bell & Howell Company
Columbus, Ohio

ISBN: 0-675-09300-7

Library of Congress Catalog Number: 70-126048

1 2 3 4 5 6 7 8 9 10 — 79 78 77 76 75 74 73 72 71 70

Printed in the United States of America

Preface

In presenting here a selection from the wealth of scholarly and critical writing about *The Sound and the Fury* I have tried to make more readily available what seemed to me most helpful to serious students of this novel. A number of different critical approaches are represented, but the emphasis is upon recent work. All selections are complete.

Two essays on this novel which should be consulted are not included here because they are available in, and are integral with, important books about Faulkner which themselves ought to be known to anyone interested in *The Sound and the Fury*. An essay by Cleanth Brooks, "Man, Time, and Eternity," a chapter in his *William Faulkner: The Yoknapatawpha Country* (New Haven: Yale University Press, 1963), is by far the best single general critical study of *The Sound and the Fury*, the one to read before reading anything else, the one to which to return after reading all others. Shorter and less comprehensive in its critical approach but still of great value is the chapter on this novel by Michael Millgate in his *The Achievement of William Faulkner* (New York: Random House, 1966), which incorporates most usefully a number of comments upon *The Sound and the Fury* made by Faulkner himself, and makes use of significant manuscript evidence.

Three other essays on this novel, contained in general books on Faulkner, should also be mentioned. The longest study of *The Sound and the Fury* yet made, one that is useful and illuminating in more ways than its title implies, is that by John W. Hunt in his *William Faulkner: Art in Theological Tension* (Syracuse, N.Y.: Syracuse University Press, 1965). An older essay which is still, like the book as a whole, worth careful reading is Olga Vickery's in her *The Novels of William Faulkner*, revised edition (Baton Rouge: Louisiana State University Press, 1964). And despite occasional inaccuracies there is much useful information on the plot, chronology, and characterization of *The Sound and the Fury* in Edmond L. Volpe, *A Reader's Guide to William Faulkner* (New York: Noonday Press, 1964).

Note on the Text

Several of the authors of the essays in this collection have revised their contributions. In addition, all essays have been edited to make certain corrections. Whenever possible, quotations and references have been verified, and factual errors corrected.

All quotations from and references to *The Sound and the Fury* have been checked against the text of the first edition (New York: Cape and Smith, 1929) and, where necessary, corrected. Page references within the essays have been changed accordingly. This 1929 first-printing, first-edition text, the most accurate yet published, has been exactly reproduced by photo-offset and reissued several times, most recently by Random House in 1966, the Modern Library in 1967. All page references to *The Sound and the Fury* in this volume, then, apply to these reissues as well as to the 1929 Cape and Smith text. (All reimpressions and reissues of this text have the same pagination, of course, p. 401 being the last page of the novel.) In addition, the text of the "Compson Appendix" which Faulkner wrote for the 1946 *Portable Faulkner* is included at the end of the 1967 Modern Library text of the novel, and all quotations from that work in this anthology refer to the 1967 Modern Library text.

James B. Meriwether

Contents

James B. Meriwether   1
   The Texual History of *The Sound and the Fury*

Walter Brylowski   33
   From "The Dark Vision: Myth in *The Sound and the Fury*"

Carvel Collins   59
   The Interior Monologues of *The Sound and the Fury*

Carvel Collins   80
   Miss Quentin's Paternity Again

Eileen Gregory   89
   Caddy Compson's World

John V. Hagopian   102
   Nihilism in Faulkner's *The Sound and the Fury*

Michel Gresset   114
   Psychological Aspects of Evil in *The Sound and the Fury*

Michael Millgate   125
   The Problem of Point of View

Richard Gunter   140
   Style and Language in *The Sound and the Fury*

The Merrill Studies
in
The Sound and the Fury

James B. Meriwether

The Textual History of
The Sound and the Fury

The publi:hing history of William Faulkner's novel *The Sound and the Fury* is not complex. The text of the original edition, published in 192ᵒ, was a careful and accurate one in most respects, and neither authorial revision nor an unusual amount of textual corruption appear to have occurred in any of the later editions and impressions in English.[1] Yet for several reasons *The Sound and the Fury* provides an opportunity for particularly useful textual study.

Revised from "Notes on the Textual History of *The Sound and the Fury*," *Papers of the Bibliographical Society of America*, 56 (Third Quarter, 1962). Reprinted by permission of the Bibliographical Society of America.

[1]There have been four separate editions (that is, separate type-settings) in America, three in England. In order of publication these are: (1) New York: Jonathan Cape and Harrison Smith, 1929; (2) London: Chatto and Windus, 1931; (3) New York: Modern Library, 1946; (4) *The Faulkner Reader* [including *The Sound and the Fury*], New York: Random House, 1954; (5) New York: New American Library (a Signet paperback), 1959; (6) London: Landsborough Publications (a Four Square paperback), 1959; (7) London: Penguin Books (a Penguin Modern Classic), 1964. The 1946 Modern Library edition (a double volume, with *As I Lay Dying*) was reissued as a Modern Library Paperback in 1954, as a Vintage book in 1961. The original 1929 text was reissued in 1966 by Random House and, with the 1946 Compson appendix, by the Modern Library in 1967.

1

The relationship between the novel and a commentary upon it which Faulkner wrote in 1945 has been often misunderstood, and the text of a widely used edition is less reliable than it should be, and is commonly assumed to be — a matter of some importance, it would seem, though the corruption involved is minor, for a book which demands so close a reading as does *The Sound and the Fury*. Probably no twentieth-century American novel has elicited more intense critical analysis, and it is obvious that we need to know as much as possible about the text of a work where every italic, every capital, every point of punctuation may carry an important burden of meaning. Careful study of the broken time-sequence of the interior monologues in the first two of the book's four sections,[2] or of its much-disputed symbolism, or of the complex, elliptical, densely textured style[3] must rest upon as firm a textual foundation as can be established. The purpose of this article is to assist the critical study of *The Sound and the Fury* by bringing together here certain information about its text, including details of its writing, of its publishing history, and of Faulkner's comments upon it.

Faulkner often referred to *The Sound and the Fury* as his own favorite among his books, the one which represented his most ambitious, uncompromising attempt at perfection in the novel, and the one which had moved him most in the writing.[4] (In the writing

---

[2] A number of attempts, none entirely successful, have been made to identify and re-arrange chronologically the various scenes and fragments in Benjy's and Quentin's sections of the novel. The most useful is that by Edmond Volpe in his *A Reader's Guide to William Faulkner,* New York: Noonday Press, 1964.

[3] One example of the danger of placing undue critical reliance upon faulty Faulkner texts occurs in *The Modern Novel in America,* by Frederick J. Hoffman, Chicago: Regnery (a Gateway paperback), 1956, pp. 178-79, where the complexity and versatility of Faulkner's style are praised, and the beginning of the fourth section of *The Sound and the Fury* is quoted as "a brilliant example of Faulkner's skill" with language. The passage is quoted from the Modern Library edition (p. 281), where it appears as two sentences plus a long, dangling fragment. But in the original Cape and Smith edition (p. 330) the passage appears as two long sentences; the dangling fragment is not a feature of Faulkner's style, but was created by a printer's error in the Modern Library edition, which substituted a period for a comma in the first sentence of the section.

[4] It is well to be cautious before accepting at face value some of Faulkner's remarks about his own and other people's work. He delighted in smoothly sidestepping questions he did not want to answer. For example, when asked in Japan which of his works did he "like the least," he replied "The one that gave me no trouble . . . was *As I Lay Dying.*" (James B. Meriwether and Michael Millgate, eds., *Lion in the Garden: Interviews with William Faulkner, 1926-1962,* New York: Random House, 1968, p. 180.) But there is abundant

rather than in the reading. Faulkner was extremely reluctant to reread his books when they were finished, and it is possible that he never read *The Sound and the Fury* again after its original publication.[5]) The fourth of his novels, it was published 7 Oct. 1929[6] by Jonathan Cape and Harrison Smith in New York, approximately a year after Faulkner had finished it, perhaps a year and a half after it had been begun.

Since there has been conflicting testimony concerning the date when Faulkner wrote it[7] and what happened to the manuscript before it was accepted by Cape and Smith,[8] it is worthwhile to determine what we can about the prepublication history of *The Sound and the Fury*. Despite some confusion about the length of time involved in writing it, there is good reason to accept the statement that Faulkner at least twice made, that it took him six months. In answer to the question "How long does it take for you to write a book?" he told a class at the University of Mississippi in 1947, according to a student who made careful notes, that the time varied — he wrote *As I Lay Dying* in six weeks, *The Sound and the Fury* in six months, and *Absalom, Absalom!* in three years.[9] Ten years

evidence that *The Sound and the Fury* meant something special to him. He described it to an audience at Virginia as his "best failure. It was the one that I anguished the most over, that I worked the hardest at, that even when I knew I couldn't bring it off, I still worked at it." (Frederick L. Gwynn and Joseph L. Blotner, eds., *Faulkner in the University: Class Conference at the University of Virginia, 1957-1958,* Charlottesville: University of Virginia Press, 1959, p. 61.) We might assume that in calling the novel a "failure," as he so often did, Faulkner was not speaking so much of his achievements as of his standards.

[5]Faulkner's last two editors at Random House, Saxe Commins and Albert Erskine, both described to me on several occasions Faulkner's reluctance to reread his earlier works, even when, as occurred during the editing of the last two volumes of the Snopes trilogy, there were compelling professional (if not artistic) reasons to do so.

[6]Publication dates of American editions of Faulkner in this article are taken from *Publishers' Weekly;* of English editions, from the *English Catalogue of Books.*

[7]An undocumented statement by Malcolm Cowley, that Faulkner wrote *The Sound and the Fury* before *Sartoris* but published it later, is the source of much of the confusion about the date of the novel. (*The Portable Faulkner,* ed. Malcolm Cowley, New York: Viking Press, 1946, p. 6.) There is no evidence for the statement (which was dropped from the revised edition of the *Portable Faulkner* in 1967), but a number of critics have accepted it — usually without acknowledging its source.

[8]Lenore Marshall, in "The Power of Words," *Saturday Review,* 28 July 1962, p. 16, recalls receiving the manuscript at the offices of Cape and Smith in 1929 after it had been rejected by thirteen other publishers, and calling it to the attention of Smith, who is alleged to have said "What's it about?" Perhaps this confusion stems from a recollection of the publishing history of Faulkner's previous novel, *Sartoris,* which may well have picked up that many rejections.

[9]*Lion in the Garden,* p. 55.

later at the University of Virginia he said that the novel had been written in the six months between the spring and fall of 1928, and that it had been "finished in all the hooraw of Smith and Hoover in November."[10]

The time when the book was written was one when personal problems had placed him under severe strain, Faulkner told Maurice Edgar Coindreau in 1937,[11] and earlier he had noted that it was conceived at a period of crisis in his career as a writer too. His third novel, *Sartoris*, had been finished in the early fall of 1927,[12] but had been rejected by Boni and Liveright, publishers of his first two novels, with whom he had a three-book contract.[13] "I believed . . . that I would never be published again. I had stopped thinking of myself in publishing terms," Faulkner wrote in 1932 of his discouragement at the continued rejection of *Sartoris* by various publishers.[14] Under these circumstances he had written *The Sound and the Fury* — "written my guts" into it, he said, "though I was not aware until the book was published that I had done so, because I had done it for pleasure." About 1933 Faulkner recalled that "When I began it I had no plan at all. I wasn't even writing a book.

---

[10]See F. L. Gwynn, "Faulkner's Raskolnikov," *Modern Fiction Studies,* IV (Summer 1958), 169n. There are errors in the table on p. 170 which gives dates of composition for Faulkner's first six novels, but although Faulkner's memory for specific dates or years was often unreliable, it seems reasonable to take seriously his statement about the span of time required by the writing; to confirm the recollection of the Hoover-Smith election, fall 1928, as the date the writing was finished, we have the corroborative evidence of the carbon typescript. However, he often gave longer spans of time in responding, in interviews, to questions about the writing of the novel. In 1955 he told Cynthia Grenier that it took him "five years of re-working and re-writing" (*Lion in the Garden,* p. 222), and two years later he told an audience at the University of Virginia "I struggled and anguished with it for a year" (*Faulkner in the University,* p. 207).

[11]Interview with M. Coindreau, May 1962. Coindreau had referred to this situation in the preface to his 1938 French translation of *The Sound and the Fury,* which he described there as "Ecrit alors que l'auteur se débattait dans des difficultés d'ordre intime" (*Le bruit et la fureur,* Paris: Gallimard, p. 14). An English translation of the preface was made by George M. Reeves, "Preface to *The Sound and the Fury,*" *Mississippi Quarterly,* XIX (Summer 1966).

[12]James B. Meriwether, *The Literary Career of William Faulkner,* Princeton: Princeton University Library, 1961, p. 65.

[13]Letter, Phil Stone to C. P. Rollins, 27 Jan. 1927. A carbon of this letter is in the Faulkner Collection of the Humanities Research Center, University of Texas. Stone states in the letter that Faulkner's three-book contract with Liveright called for a $200 advance on the first book, with $400 in advance on the next two.

[14]Faulkner, introduction to the Modern Library issue of *Sanctuary* (New York, 1932), p. vi.

I was thinking of books, publication, only in the reverse, in saying to myself, I wont have to worry about publishers liking or not liking this at all." One day, he said, after *Sartoris* had been turned down again and again, "I seemed to shut a door between me and all publishers' addresses and book lists. I said to myself, Now I can write. Now I can make myself a vase like that which the old Roman kept at his bedside and wore the rim slowly away with kissing it. So I, who had never had a sister and was fated to lose my daughter in infancy, set out to make myself a beautiful and tragic little girl."[15]

Years later, Faulkner's old friend Phil Stone, the Oxford lawyer who was so close to him, and who did so much for him, during the first part of his career, recalled that Faulkner had told him nothing about *The Sound and the Fury* until it was finished. Although he had kept in close touch with Stone during the writing of *Sartoris*, Stone had not even known he was writing anything until the completion of *The Sound and the Fury*.[16] But afterward came the experience, still cherished by Stone, of sitting "night after night in Bill's little room in the little tower of the old Delta Psi chapter house" at the University of Mississippi while Faulkner read aloud *The Sound and the Fury* to him page by page.[17]

Presumably it was the original manuscript, not his later typescript, that Faulkner read to Stone in Mississippi, for it was in New York, in his friend (and literary agent) Ben Wasson's room on Macdougal Street, opposite the Provincetown Playhouse, that Faulkner completed typing the novel. According to Wasson, Faulkner brought the manuscript to New York and there typed the final version himself.[18] On the last page of the carbon which he bound and retained for his files, Faulkner added by hand, at the end of the typed text, the place and the date: "New York, N.Y. | October 1928."[19] Wasson recalls that when he finished it, Faulkner offered him the whole typescript with the words "Read this, Bud. It's a real sonofabitch."[20]

---

[15]*Literary Career,* p. 16; Michael Millgate, *The Achievement of William Faulkner,* New York: Random House, 1966, p. 26. See below for a more extensive discussion of the typescript — apparently a version of an unpublished introduction Faulkner wrote for *The Sound and the Fury* — from which these quotations are taken.
[16]Interview with Mr. Stone, July 1956.
[17]Letter, Phil Stone to James B. Meriwether, 7 July 1960.
[18]Interview with Mr. Wasson, September 1959.
[19]*Literary Career,* p. 65.
[20]Interview with Mr. Wasson, September 1959.

In addition to a carbon of his final typescript, Faulkner preserved among his papers a manuscript, lacking only one page of being complete.[21] As was his custom, he used thin sheets of legal-size paper, leaving a wide left-hand margin for corrections.[22] A page-by-page comparison, with spot collation, of manuscript, carbon typescript, and published book reveals that each version follows the previous one closely, though with a great deal of verbal polishing and minor revision from manuscript to typescript, and a certain amount of further polishing from typescript to published book. The manuscript itself gives evidence of very extensive rewriting, with many passages added, some canceled, and with its pagination revealing that many of the pages Faulkner preserved represent revisions and expansions of previous ones.[23] Apparently the manuscript represents finished work, Faulkner not troubling to preserve anything prior to it. In typing it out in New York, Faulkner inevitably gave it a certain amount of revising, and at some point after this typing revised it yet further, producing the differences between the carbon typescript and the finished book either by later changes in the ribbon copy (which presumably went to the publisher and eventually became printer's setting copy) or by changes in the proofs.

One or more complete drafts, or none; extensive working notes, or none, may have preceded the extant manuscript but not have been preserved. For this particular novel, we might well suppose such measures a necessity; for this particular novelist, we may well asume that they were not.[24] In the case of another work in which there are complex dislocations of time, *A Fable*, we know that

---

[21]*Literary Career*, p. 65. The missing page is no. 5.

[22]Pages of this manuscript have been reproduced as follows: pp. 34, 70, 148 in *Literary Career*, Figs. 10 and 11, and in the *Princeton University Library Chronicle*, XVIII (Spring 1957), Plate III; the first page in Linton R. Massey, "Man Working," *1919—1962 . . . A Catalogue of the William Faulkner Collections at the University of Virginia*, Charlottesville: Bibliographical Society of the University of Virginia, 1968, p. 36.

[23]The first critical discussion of the novel to benefit from a study of this manuscript is that of Michael Millgate in his *The Achievement of William Faulkner*, which includes a number of quotations from it. Further quotations from the manuscript of Benjy's section are contained in Emily K. Izsak, "The Manuscript of *The Sound and the Fury*: The Revisions in the First Section," *Studies in Bibliography*, XX (1967).

[24]Faulkner often stated that *As I Lay Dying* had been a *tour de force* in conception and execution—"I knew when I put down the first word what the last word . . . would be," he said at Virginia in 1957 (*Faulkner in the University*, p. 207). Though *As I Lay Dying* is a much shorter and simpler novel than *The Sound and the Fury*, it will not do to underestimate the capacities of the mind that so completely conceived it before the writing began. In the introduction to the Modern Library *Sanctuary* he made the statement that

Faulkner used such notes, putting on the wall of his study a day-by-day chronology of the action of the novel.[25] But when in Japan in 1955 he was twice asked if he had worked from notes in writing the first section of *The Sound and the Fury*, he once ignored the question, once replied with a curt "No." We might be tempted to agree with the unbelief of the questioner who on that occasion stated, "I made a thorough study of the first section and I felt that it was humanly impossible to write it down from the very beginning without any notes," and Faulkner did admit to his Japanese audience that he occasionally used such notes, throwing them away when he was through with them.[26] But lacking proof to the contrary it seems unwise to assume that Faulkner could not have constructed the novel in his head and set it down without working notes, even if he did not do so in the case of *A Fable*.[27]

If Faulkner "had no plan at all" when he sat down to write at this time, save the ambition to create for himself something moving and imperishable, he did have in mind when he began writing a basic image which was to dominate the work. This was "the picture of the little girl's [Caddy's] muddy drawers," as she climbed the pear tree to look in the window while her brothers waited below.[28] But Faulkner conceived it as a short story before it became a novel. As he said in Japan in 1955, it

> began as a short story, it was a story without plot, of some children being sent away from the house during the grandmother's funeral ... and then the idea struck me to see how much more I could have

---

As I Lay Dying had been written "in six weeks, without changing a word." As George Garrett has shown ("Some Revisions in *As I Lay Dying*," *Modern Language Notes,* 73 [June 1958], 414-17), the novel actually underwent a good deal of minor polishing and revision at every stage, from manuscript to typescript to printed book. It will not do, then, to take too literally the words of the *Sanctuary* introduction (which Faulkner often repeated elsewhere). One logical way of taking the statement would be to assume that Faulkner expected sensible readers to understand that the book could not possibly have been written literally "without changing a word," and was using this way — a by no means uncharacteristic blend of honesty, modesty, and ambiguity — to call attention to his quite extraordinary feat of concentration and control in the planning and writing.

[25]*Life*, 9 August 1954, pp. 77-78, and James W. Webb, "Faulkner Writes *A Fable*," *University of Mississippi Studies in English*, VII (1966).

[26]*Lion in the Garden*, 146, 147, 145.

[27]One reason that Faulkner may well have followed a different procedure in writing *A Fable* is that it took him much longer than did *The Sound and the Fury*. At the end of *A Fable* (New York: Random House, 1954, p. 437) Faulkner gave December 1944 as the date it was begun, November 1953 as the date it was finished.

[28]*Faulkner in the University*, p. 1.

got out of the idea of the blind, self-centeredness of innocence, typified by children, if one of those children had been truly innocent, that is, an idiot. So the idiot was born and then I became interested in the relationship of the idiot to the world that he was in but would never be able to cope with and just where could he get the tenderness, the help, to shield him in his innocence. . . . And so the character of his sister began to emerge, then the brother, who . . . represented complete evil . . . appeared. Then it needs the protagonist, someone to tell the story, so Quentin appeared. By that time I found out I couldn't possibly tell that in a short story. . . .

So the novel grew, Faulkner said, with the three brothers each permitted to tell their version of the story, "and then I had to write another section from the outside . . . to tell what had happened on that particular day."[29]

When Faulkner showed the completed typescript of the novel to Ben Wasson in the fall of 1928 he remarked that he did not expect it to be published,[30] and it was in fact rejected by Harcourt, Brace. But Harrison Smith, who as an editor at Harcourt, Brace had been influential in the firm's decision to accept *Sartoris* earlier that fall,[31] had in the meantime set up in the publishing business himself, and he decided to gamble upon the book, and its author,[32] though he warned Faulkner when he accepted it that *The Sound and the Fury* would not sell.[33]

The new firm of Cape and Smith published its first book, Evelyn Scott's Civil War novel *The Wave*, on 1 July 1929.[34] At about that time Faulkner wrote from Pascagoula, Mississippi, a letter about the proofs — presumably the galley proofs — of *The Sound and the Fury*, which he had just corrected. His letter was in reply to one from Wasson, who had joined the Cape and Smith staff as an assis-

[29]*Lion in the Garden,* pp. 146-147. In 1937 Faulkner gave M. E. Coindreau the same account of the book's inception as a short story (*Le bruit et la fureur,* p. 7).
[30]Interview with Mr. Wasson, Sept. 1959.
[31]Interview with Mr. Wasson, Aug. 1957.
[32]According to Wasson, Smith knew about *The Sound and the Fury* when still at Harcourt, Brace. Some time after he had left to set up his own business, knowing that *The Sound and the Fury* had been submitted to them, he sent Wasson to Harcourt, Brace to ask what had happened. Wasson was told that the book had been rejected, and he brought the typescript back to Smith himself (telephone conversation with Mr. Wasson, July 1962).
[33]Faulkner, introduction to Modern Library *Sanctuary,* p. vi. The contract with Cape and Smith was signed 18 Feb. 1929 (information supplied from records at Random House, Mar. 1957, by Saxe Commins).
[34]*Publishers' Weekly,* 13 July 1929, p. 207.

tant editor,[35] and who seems to have made certain editorial changes in the first section of the book which Faulkner, in correcting the proofs, had restored to his original readings.

Wasson had apparently copy edited the interior monologue of Benjy, the idiot, which opens the book, in order to indicate the breaks in time sequence by means of wider spacing between lines in the text, instead of adhering to Faulkner's original system (which appears in both the manuscript and the typescript he preserved) of indicating these shifts by means of a change from roman to italic type, or back from italic to roman. Presumably Wasson had argued that the italic-roman shift was unsatisfactory because it indicated only two time-levels, but that at least four different dates were involved; Faulkner, replying with typical brevity, clarity, and force, argued first that the breaks were no more effective than the type-shift in indicating change, and recalled twice the number of distinct time-levels:

> Dear Ben —
> Thank you for the letter.
> I received the proof. It seemed pretty tough to me, so I corrected it as written, adding a few more italics where the original seemed obscure on second reading. Your reason for the change, i.e., that with italics only 2 different dates were indicated I do not think sound for 2 reasons. First, I do not see that the use of breaks clarifies it any more; second, there are more than 4 dates involved. The ones I recall off-hand are: Damuddy dies. Benjy is 3. (2) His name is changed. He is 5. (3) Caddy's wedding. He is 14. (4) He tries to rape a young girl and is castrated. 15. (5) Quentin's death. (6) The father's death. (7) A visit to the cemetary at 18. (7) The day of the anecdote, he is 33. These are just a few I recall, so your reason explodes itself.

Faulkner went on to defend his system on broader grounds, but also reminded Wasson that his own preference, as he had once (presumably when he had been in New York the previous fall) proposed to Wasson and Smith, was for printing the section in inks of different colors:

> But the main reason is, a break indicates an objective change in tempo, while the objective picture here should be a continuous whole, since the thought transference is subjective; i.e., in Ben's

---

[35]*Publishers' Weekly*, 23 Feb. 1929, p. 880.

mind and not in the reader's eye. I think italics are necessary to
establish for the reader Benjy's confusion; that unbroken-surfaced
confusion of an idiot which is outwardly a dynamic and logical
coherence. To gain this, by using breaks it will be necessary to write
an induction for each transference. I wish publishing was advanced
enough to use colored ink for such, as I argued with you and Hal
in the speak-easy that day. But the form in which you now have it
is pretty tough. It presents a most dull and poorly articulated
picture to my eye. If something must be done, it were better to
re-write this whole section objectively, like the 4th section. I think
it is rotten, as is. But if you wont have it so, I'll just have to save
the idea until publishing grows up to it. Anyway, change all the.
italics. You overlooked one of them. Also, the parts written in
italics will all have to be punctuated again. You'd better see to that,
since you're all for coherence. And dont make any more additions
to the script, bud. I know you mean well, but so do I. I effaced the
2 or 3 you made.

After a few sentences on other subjects, Faulkner returned to the
editing of his book with a final paragraph devoted to a restatement
of his position. It was not the first time — and by no means was to
be the last time — that the editing of one of his books was characterized by ignorance of or indifference to his own methods and
intentions; the first and last sentences of the paragraph are a plea
he might have addressed to any of his editors:

> I hope you will think better of this. Your reason above disproves
> itself. I purposely used italics for both actual scenes and remem-
> bered scenes for the reason, not to indicate the different dates of
> happenings, but merely to permit the reader to anticipate a thought-
> transference, letting the recollection postulate its own date. Surely
> you see this.
>
> Bill[36]

It is obvious from this letter that Faulkner, a proud and in some
ways supremely confident craftsman, was thoroughly aware of the
difficulties in design and printing caused by his book, and it is
interesting to see that he could entertain the idea of several radically different solutions to these problems in Benjy's section. His
decisive rejection of the possibility of indicating the time shifts by

---

[36]See *"Man Working"*, pp. 106-107, for a reproduction of the entire letter. It
is quoted by Millgate in his excellent discussion of the novel (*Achievement*,
pp. 93-94).

breaks in the text is revealing. A writer who would admit the possibility of rewriting the whole section in the third person, or of writing a new induction or beginning to each new time sequence, can hardly be called inflexible in his thinking about the book, and his two reasons for rejecting the breaks in the text have important implications. His concern with book design appears both in his argument that the breaks in the type page were displeasing to the eye, and in his explanation that such a break would distort the impression he was trying to give of the real confusion of time in the idiot's mind, a confusion that Faulkner wanted to emphasize by the seeming continuity of his interior monologue. Such concern is not surprising in an author who had several times during the past decade made up little booklets of his verse, fiction, or drama, doing all the illustrating, lettering, and binding himself.[37] One of them, "Mayday," has drawings in color by Faulkner, and though he early discovered that he wrote better than he drew,[38] and though he apparently never attempted to illustrate his serious mature work, he had a natural interest in the Blakean combination of picture and word, which helps explain his anxiety that the design in type of the Benjy section should match as closely as possible his conception of the idiot's associative thought processes. We can imagine that Faulkner deeply regretted the possibility of achieving this by printing in colors, and since he proposed such differing alternative methods of handling the problem, we can imagine too his satisfaction when *The Sound and the Fury* eventually attained a certain degree of popular as well as critical success and so confirmed the validity of the method he had insisted upon in 1929. In 1955 he was asked his present opinion of his original idea of using ink of various colors, and he replied that his "original fear that the reader might need such a device seems not to have been valid," and that he now had "no desire to see the novel so printed."[39]

---

[37]He made several copies of one of these, the play "The Marionettes," about 1920. A page from one is reproduced in *Literary Career,* Fig. 1. "Mayday," a later work, is described briefly by Carvel Collins in the introduction to his edition of Faulkner's *New Orleans Sketches,* New York: Random House, 1968, p. xxx.

[38]In 1925 he praised, not without envy, the skill of his artist friend William Spratling, "whose hand has been shaped to a brush as mine has (alas!) not. . . ." (*New Orleans Sketches,* p. 46.) The best of Faulkner's drawings are far from contemptible in design and execution, however, and as one would expect, even the poorer ones have individuality, even those so reminiscent of Beardsley and Held.

[39]Quoted by John Cook Wylie in the *Richmond News Leader,* 31 Jan. 1955, p. 11.

It would be extremely interesting to see a set of the galley proofs of the book, were a set ever to turn up. It seems possible that certain slightly puzzling or inconsistent points in the first section of the published book may be due to editorial changes which Faulkner overlooked in reading the proofs, or corrected inconsistently. His letter makes it clear that he left to an editorial hand the job of repunctuating (i.e., restoring to the original typescript punctuation) the italic passages, and this may well have been carried out with less than total fidelity to Faulkner's intentions.

What the first few proofsheets of the book looked like before Faulkner corrected them may be inferred from an examination of a printer's sample octavo gathering (title-page, copyright page, and first fourteen pages of text) for *The Sound and the Fury* now in the Faulkner collection of the Humanities Research Center of the University of Texas. (See illustration.)[40] In the published book the first italic passage occurs on p. 3. On p. 3 of the sample gathering the passage appears in roman type, leaded out to form a gap of between one and two lines' width at the beginning and ending of the passage. With one exception, the remaining italic passages in the first fourteen pages of the published book (including the two fragments on lines 6 and 8 of p. 8) all appear in roman, with the breaks, in the sample gathering. The exception — one wonders why — is the second of the italic passages in the book, that on p. 5. As Faulkner told Wasson, the leading out creates an ugly type page and a disruption of the reader's experience of Benjy's interior monologue.

To assist in publicizing the novel, Cape and Smith sent a set of the galleys (Wasson recalls that she returned them) to Evelyn Scott for comment, since *The Wave* had become something of a critical and popular success. She responded so enthusiastically in a letter that Wasson asked her to revise and expand her remarks, particularly on the Benjy section. She did this, and her commentary was issued in a little pamphlet, its cover carrying out the black-and-white design of the covers of the novel, which was distributed along with the book.[41] Paperbound prepublication copies were also

---

[40]For permission to reproduce this material, thanks are due to Random House, Faulkner's publisher in this country, and to the Humanities Research Center of the University of Texas.

[41]Evelyn Scott, *On William Faulkner's "The Sound and the Fury." Publishers' Weekly,* 21 Sept. 1929, p. 1138, carried a statement by Cape and Smith in their announcement of fall books that "After reading the galleys of this remarkable book, EVELYN SCOTT wrote us enthusiastically, 'His idiot is better than Dostoyevsky's!' " Other information from interview with Mr. Wasson, Sept. 1959.

circulated. All in all, Cape and Smith were to be congratulated on the way they brought out a novel which represented a considerable gamble for a new firm. It was published 7 Oct. 1929, an autumn for greater optimism concerning America's literary than financial condition, and received very good reviews, upon the whole; but it did not sell. The first printing, only 1,789 copies, sufficed until the publication of *Sanctuary* in February 1931. In that month a small second printing of 518 copies was made, and the following November a third printing, of 1,000 copies, was made from a copy of the second impression by offset lithography.[42]

The final printing of 1,000 copies appears to have lasted several successive publishers for more than a decade. By the late fall of 1931 Cape and Smith were out of business, to be succeeded, as Faulkner's publishers, first by Smith and Haas, then by Random House. The volumes of the *Publisher's Trade List Annual* recorded the continued availability, at $2.50, of *The Sound and the Fury* from Smith and Haas through 1935, and from Random House from 1936 through 1943.

Granted the exceptional difficulty of the text, the complications caused by a number of individual or idiosyncratic features of Faulkner's spelling and punctuation, the distance of author from publisher, and the inconsistencies of copy editing noted by Faulkner in his letter to Wasson, it would have been a small miracle had the text of the first edition of *The Sound and the Fury* been less imperfect than it actually was. Despite a certain number of demonstrable minor printer's errors and inconsistencies, and a larger number of possible or debatable ones, it is on the whole a very good text, and much better than any of the later editions.

---

[42]Dates of printing appear on the copyright pages of the second and third impressions. For the number of copies in all three printings, I am indebted to Mrs. Evelyn Harter Glick, formerly of Cape and Smith, and of Smith and Haas, who collected the information with the intention of publishing a Faulkner bibliography in collaboration with Kenneth Godfrey. (The project, begun with great thoroughness, was unfortunately abandoned sometime in 1932.) Mrs. Glick also provided, from the Cape and Smith records, the information that no textual changes were made in the second and third impressions, a fact confirmed by both oral and machine collation, though in the third printing commas were inserted between the date of the month and the year in the headings of the second, third, and fourth sections. For their assistance with the task of collating these impressions, and also the texts of the Modern Library, Chatto and Windus, and *Faulkner Reader* editions, I wish to thank Mrs. Mary C. Bozeman, Mr. James B. Davis, Miss Margaret Meriwether, and Mrs. Nancy C. Meriwether.

"Wait a minute." Luster said. "You snagged on that nail again. Cant you never crawl through here without snagging on that nail."

Caddy uncaught me and we crawled through. Uncle Maury said to not let anybody see us, so we better stoop over, Caddy said. Stoop over, Benjy. Like this, see. We stooped over and crossed the garden, where the flowers rasped and rattled against us. The ground was hard. We climbed the fence, where the pigs were grunting and snuffing. I expect they're sorry because one of them got killed today, Caddy said. The ground was hard, churned and knotted.

Keep your hands in your pockets, Caddy said. Or they'll get froze. You dont want your hands froze on Christmas, do you.

"It's too cold out there." Versh said. "You dont want to go out doors."

"What is it now." Mother said.

"He want to go out doors." Versh said.

"Let him go." Uncle Maury said.

"It's too cold." Mother said. "He'd better stay in. Benjamin. Stop that, now."

"It wont hurt him." Uncle Maury said.

"You, Benjamin." Mother said. "If you dont be good, you'll have to go to the kitchen."

3

Page 3 of the sample gathering (1929) of *The Sound and the Fury*.

Reproduced by courtesy of Random House, Inc., and of the University of Texas.

"Wait a minute." Luster said. "You snagged on that nail again. Cant you never crawl through here without snagging on that nail."

Caddy uncaught me and we crawled through. Uncle Maury said to not let anybody see us, so we better stoop over, Caddy said. Stoop over, Benjy. Like this, see. We stooped over and crossed the garden, where the flowers rasped and rattled against us. The ground was hard. We climbed the fence, where the pigs were grunting and snuffing. I expect they're sorry because one of them got killed today, Caddy said. The ground was hard, churned and knotted.

Keep your hands in your pockets, Caddy said. Or they'll get froze. You don't want your hands froze on Christmas, do you.

"It's too cold out there." Versh said. "You dont want to go out doors."

"What is it now." Mother said.

"He want to go out doors." Versh said.

"Let him go." Uncle Maury said.

"It's too cold." Mother said. "He'd better stay in. Benjamin. Stop that, now."

"It wont hurt him." Uncle Maury said.

"You, Benjamin." Mother said. "If you dont be good, you'll have to go to the kitchen."

"Mammy say keep him out the kitchen today." Versh said. "She say she got all that cooking to get done."

3

Listed below in Table A are the obvious or demonstrable errors in the 1929 Cape and Smith edition. It is noteworthy how few misspellings due to printer's errors there are; for a careful collation to turn up only one obvious typo (that on p. 216) in a novel of 400 pages is an indication of careful printing and proofreading. Since Faulkner varied his usage, from section to section and even within the section, depending upon the state of mind of the subject of the interior monologue, it is not at all surprising that there are real inconsistencies, as well as apparent ones, in matters of punctuation, the handling of direct quotations, and the use of apostrophes. For example, it would seem that Faulkner intended to indicate something about the quality of Benjy's perception of the world about him by uniformly omitting the question marks in the questions that are asked in the dialogue of his section of the novel. Akin to this device, but not employed with complete consistency, is the separation of dialogue from its adjunctive "he said" and "she said" by periods, instead of commas. That is, Benjy's mind appears to be recording the finality of a statement, in dialogue, by putting a period at the end of the statement; its connection to the following "he said" appears only in the lower case letter of the "he." But where there is inconsistency in the practice, is Faulkner attempting to indicate some subtle difference in the situation, or Benjy's perception of it, or did copy editor or printer make a change? Again, it seems obvious that nothing but errors of commission by printers, omission by proofreaders, are involved in the occasional appearance in one-syllable contractions like *wont* of the apostrophes which Faulkner, it is clear from his manuscripts and typescripts, prefers to omit. But it is less clear what is involved in the occasional omission of apostrophes in two-syllable contractions like *wouldn't;* some of them appear to be meaningless omissions, others might just possibly be related to the changes of punctuation that appear in the italicized passages of Benjy's and Quentin's sections.

Other problems in the text of this novel, as in other books by Faulkner, occur from his preference for omitting the periods after the contractions Mr., Mrs., and Dr.; his preference for occasional *-our* forms *(humour, labouring)* and the *-ise* ending for certain verbs (do these reflect the author's taste for earlier American forms, or more recent English practice?); his liking for *awhile* and *anymore* instead of *a while* and *any more;* and so on. There is even one apparently deliberate Gallicism: *quai* for *quay.*

In a work where symbolism, imagery, and literary allusions are so densely, and often so inconspicuously, woven into the texture of the prose, a high degree of editorial conservatism would be called for if a new edition of the novel were to be brought out now. Consistency might mistakenly urge the smoothing out of spelling, punctuation, and other features of the style which could significantly enrich the reader's understanding of a particular passage, but it is obvious that certain inconsistencies are almost sure to be the fault of the printer and copy editor. Wherever the context, or

TABLE A[43]

ERRORS IN THE 1929 EDITION OF *The Sound and the Fury*

page and line	error	suggested correction	page and line	error	suggested correction
3.15	*don't*	*dont*	196.3	we'll	well
9.3	don't	dont	197.7	I'll	Ill
9.24	baby," she	baby." she	200.28	he'll	hell
10.1	Don't	Dont	202.12	I'm	Im
10.25	Don't	Dont	216.16	*Nom sum*	*Non sum*
11.8	Can't	Cant	233.16	She	she
30.20	said,	said.	240.29	enevelope	envelope
33.20	barn.	barn."	252.20	don't	dont
38.13	don't	dont	260.12	can't	cant
38.14	*can't*	*cant*	263.4	start.	start,
38.19	go,"	go."	270.13	o'clock	oclock
43.23	said,	said.	273.4	childrens'	children's
48.10	up"	up."	286.22	can't	cant
56.28	Benjy,"	Benjy."	292.22	don't	dont
74.22	*Benjy.*	*Benjy,*	295.18	can't	cant
75.5	Mr.	Mr	322.11	o'clock	oclock
84.5	fast,	fast.	324.2	He	"He
86.11	up,	up.	328.7	don't	dont
125.12	hear?	hear?"	343.10	He	he
125.17	o'clock	oclock	346.16	Cahline	Miss Cahline
130.22	girls	girl's	347.14	you alls'	you all's
156.25	again,	again.	355.9	beatin'	beatin
168.1	You	"You	357.14	here?"	here."
179.15	weetha.	weetha."	357.17	here?	here?"
185.16	Geralds	Gerald's	369.13	!	!"
188.9	I've	Ive	393.21	somethin'	somethin
190.11	I'll	Ill	394.10	said.	said,

---

[43]As printed here this table omits fifteen "errors" which were included in the original version but which now appear to me to fall into a category of probably acceptable inconsistencies which there is no real need to correct. (An example is the word "jeweler" at 105.7, which is spelled "jeweller" elsewhere.) A full study of Faulkner's manuscript and typescript, even without the evidence of the missing galleys, would probably solve these and other textual problems that would need investigation for a definitive edition of the novel; in the meantime their persistence in the text is unlikely to affect its interpretation.

comparison with prevailing practice elsewhere in the book, argue very strongly that the inconsistency is not substantive, it is listed here in Table A. Other cases are ignored, for though it is to be hoped that this table will shed light upon the textual problems of this novel, a more thorough investigation of the whole text must involve collation of the published version with the extant manuscript and typescript texts. Only such a collation would reveal whether such occasionally disturbing inconsistencies, not listed here, as the use of apostrophes in contractions, in the punctuation, and in the use of italics are the fault of the author, or are due to slipshod copy editing and proofreading.

In April, 1931 the first English edition of *The Sound and the Fury* was brought out in London by Chatto and Windus, in a printing of 2,000 copies.[44] Faulkner's second book to be published in England (it followed *Soldiers' Pay* by less than a year), it had an introduction by Richard Hughes, who praised highly the novel's technique and structure. These produce, he said, an effect "impossible to describe . . . because it is unparalleled," and he noted particularly the "exquisite care" that had been used in fitting together the pattern of Benjy's section, the parts of which had been written with such "consummate contrapuntal skill."

English readers might have had more confidence in Faulkner's skill if they had been given a better text by which to judge it. When Chatto and Windus brought out *Sanctuary* the following fall, they censored the novel by omitting 325 words, but in other respects did a more careful job of printing it than had been done in America, where it had been somewhat sloppily copy edited and proofread.[45] However, the English edition of *The Sound and the Fury* was indifferently copy edited, little consistency being exhibited in the many departures made from the original text in spelling and punctuation, and although only a few printer's errors can be identified as such, some of the many changes in the original punctuation probably should be attributed to this source rather than to the copy editing.

House styling and other changes of the sort that almost invariably occur when an American book is set up in Britain (or a British book in America) account for many, perhaps the majority, of the

---

[44]Meriwether, *Literary Career*, p. 102. This edition appears not to have been reprinted until the 1954 "Uniform Edition" text was reproduced by photo-offset from the original impression.
[45]James B. Meriwether, "Some Notes on the Text of Faulkner's *Sanctuary*," *Papers of the Bibliographical Society of America*, 55 (Third Quarter, 1961), 203-5.

differences between the first English and first American editions of the novel. There are the usual Anglicizations of spelling: *parlour*, *ploughed, draught, tyre*. Though *gasoline* does not become *petrol*, and *curb* remains *curb*, *motor* is substituted for *auto*. Such changes exaggerate the inconsistencies in the American text caused by Faulkner's occasional use of English forms. More serious is the fact that a number of Faulkner's dialectal or colloquial words and expressions are modified (some perhaps by printer rather than editor): for *hit, bein, nothin, shamed, begun, belong at* are substituted *it, being, nothing, ashamed, began, belong to*. Apostrophes are inserted (with less than perfect consistency) in Faulkner's *cant*, *wont, dont*, and after *Mr* and *Mrs* periods are usually supplied. Hyphens are added to many compounds: thus *drug store* becomes *drug-store, woodlot* becomes *wood-lot*. Trivial in themselves, these changes are all away from Faulkner's practice of eliminating punctuation that breaks up or slows down the movement of the eye across the type page unless demanded by the meaning (rather than the form) of the words. And though again it is not carried through with any degree of consistency, a further modification of Faulkner's practice in this respect is the addition of apostrophes to indicate omission of unpronounced letters in spoken words: *'tis, makin'*, *S'pose*. The *-ise* verb ending so often preferred by Faulkner is changed to *-ize*: *civilized, criticize, fertilizing, realize, recognize*.

The greatest number of changes in the English edition are in punctuation. As we have seen, inconsistencies in the American edition afford some justification for this, and if the changes by Chatto and Windus had eliminated some of the American inconsistencies there would be little ground for complaint. Unfortunately the changes produced less consistency, not more, and despite many dozens of alterations, the result is a less respectable text. Commas are inserted, commas are omitted; periods are exchanged for commas, and vice versa.

Although the great majority of the changes made in the English edition of the novel do not affect the basic meaning of the passages in which they occur, in sum they unquestionably mar the text of the work, particularly since most of them were made inconsistently. The English reader misses a good many of the finer shades of pronunciation and rhythm in the dialogue through changes made in spelling and punctuation. He loses the chance of the closer acquaintance with Faulkner's mind which familiarity with some of the little idiosyncrasies of usage in the American text afford. And perhaps worst of all, the inconsistencies caused by careless copy editing and proofreading are apt to shake the reader's confidence in his text, and to discourage the kind of close attention the writing deserves. There are also a few ordinary typographical errors. These are listed in Table B below more for the light they shed on the printing and proofreading of the book than because of their importance, though in one or two instances there is significant change in the meaning of the sentence in which the error occurs. Page and line references are to the first English and first American editions. (A number of possible errors in the dialogue are not listed because conceivably they could represent editorial modification of dialect.)

TABLE B

ERRORS IN THE FIRST ENGLISH EDITION OF *The Sound and the Fury*

English		American	
14.26	They they	18.13	Then they
19.26	fell	24.28	I fell
26.30	Gid	34.1	Git
48.2	I have just to	60.25	I just have to
71.12	unbottoned	89.29	unbuttoned
93.33	Will	117.27	Was. Will
107.28	necessarily	134.26	unnecessarily
127.9	Dog	159.13	Doc
131.22	shiny	164.28	shiny tight
135.2	go	169.8	go back
171.6	*girl*	213.25	*girl Girl*
175.23	and it	219.19	and i it
191.14	in	238.23	on
207.17	'is,	258.13	is,"
212.4	shes ays	264.4	she says
216.25	your own	269.24	your
227.25	arrangement	283.17	agreement
260.32	next	325.10	about next
291.9	cycamores	363.5	sycamores
313.15	you.	391.7	you."

One of the most interesting chapters in the publishing history of *The Sound and the Fury* concerns the special edition of the novel which Random House proposed to bring out in 1933. Beginning with his ninth novel, *Absalom, Absalom!*, in 1936, Random House became Faulkner's publishers for all his books, but his connection with the firm dates from several years earlier. In 1931 they had brought out one of his short stories, *Idyll in the Desert*, in a little limited edition signed by the author, and early in 1932 they issued *Sanctuary*, with a special introduction by Faulkner, in their low-priced

Modern Library series. It may have been the success of these two projects which encouraged Random House to contemplate bringing out *The Sound and the Fury* in a new, limited edition with an introduction by the author.

In this edition the first section was to be printed in ink of various colors to help clarify the chronology, as Faulkner had proposed when the novel was first published, and for it he underlined his copy of the book in crayon of different colors and sent it, with the introduction, to Random House.[46] The 1933 *Publishers' Trade List Annual* carried a Random House "tentative advance announcement for the fall of 1933" which listed "A new limited Edition" of *The Sound and the Fury*, "With a new introduction by William Faulkner. Typography by the Grabhorn Press. 500 copies, signed by William Faulkner. Ready in November. $7.50."

Random House deserves great credit for even contemplating such a project during depression times, for it would have entailed a heavy printing bill indeed. But though the edition was announced again in the 1934 *Trade List Annual* for fall, 1934, publication, it was abandoned before completion. No trace of either Faulkner's introduction or the copy of the book with the crayon underlining can now be found at Random House.[47]

Reference has already been made to the incomplete, four-page typescript among Faulkner's papers which appears to be a draft of his introduction for this edition, and it is worth further comment here. The first page is lacking. The second begins in mid-sentence with a reference to the reading he had done a decade and more before he wrote *Sanctuary* but from which he was still learning. In writing *Sanctuary*, and later *As I Lay Dying*, he noted, he had found something missing from the experience that writing *The Sound and the Fury* had been. This — a feeling hard to define but including an actual physical emotion, faith and joy and ecstasy and an eager looking forward to what the process of creation would release from the paper before him — this, he felt, might have been

---

[46]In a letter to Malcolm Cowley, written late in 1945, Faulkner referred to this as a project of "About 10 years ago . . . using different color inks to clarify chronology, etc." For it, Faulkner stated, he had sent a copy of the book, "underlined . . . in different color crayons," to Bennett Cerf at Random House. (Malcolm Cowley, ed. *The Faulkner-Cowley File,* New York: Viking Press, 1966, p. 45.) Though the letter does not state that it is the first section which was so underlined, I assume that this is the case, since elsewhere Faulkner indicated that it was only this section which he conceived would benefit from printing in color. (*Lion in the Garden,* p. 147.)

[47]Information supplied by Albert Erskine, November 1961.

missing with *As I Lay Dying* because he had known so much about that book before writing it. He waited nearly two years before beginning his next novel, and then tried to recreate for *Light in August* the conditions of writing *The Sound and the Fury*, by sitting down to face the first blank sheet with only a single image in mind instead of the whole book, in this case the image of a pregnant girl making her way along an unfamiliar road.

But the new novel failed to bring him the feeling he had had with *The Sound and the Fury*, though it progressed satisfactorily. Realizing that he had now become a far more conscious, deliberate craftsman, more aware of the standards and achievements of his great predecessors among novelists in French and English, he wondered if he were not now in the situation of knowing too much about the techniques of fiction, and if he had not already made use of the only image, that of Caddy in her muddy drawers trying to see the funeral from the pear tree while her brothers waited below, which had the power to move him as he wanted the act of writing to do.

Faulkner concluded the piece with the description already quoted of the writing of *The Sound and the Fury*, of putting out of his mind the disappointment engendered by his failure to place the manuscript of *Sartoris*, and setting out to make himself "a beautiful and tragic little girl."

Though we cannot be absolutely certain that this was designed for the introduction to the 1933 limited edition of *The Sound and the Fury*, it fits in date and in scope, as far as we can tell from the internal (and incomplete) evidence of the typescript itself, and it is difficult to imagine anything else that it would fit. It is altogether a remarkably self-revelatory piece, for Faulkner; it is equally far in tone and attitude from the protective mask of tough, hard-boiled cynicism he had worn in introducing a lesser work, *Sanctuary*, a short time before, and from the pose of being an untutored rustic, or ignorant natural genius, which he was already finding useful.

Even with the lack of the first page, this is an important document for the understanding of its author. The picture it gives of Faulkner the widely read, ambitious, consecrated artist makes it tempting to speculate what might have been the effect of the publication of such an introduction with a beautifully prepared and printed Random House-Grabhorn Press edition of *The Sound and the Fury* in the 1930's. It seems reasonable to suppose that it might have changed radically, perhaps effaced, the picture which so many of his American readers derived from an unperceptive reading of *Sanctuary* and its Modern Library introduction. The whole course of the reception of his books in this country might have been swayed, not so much perhaps in the direction of winning for him a larger audience, but at any rate of producing a better one. Instead, misapprehensions about Faulkner the man went far toward confirming a certain fashionable condescension toward his work which prevailed for long in the literary circles of America, and which encouraged too many readers and too many critics in a superficial approach to his fiction. (As a French admirer of Faulkner put it in 1938, comparing the relative popularity of *Sanctuary* and *The Sound and the Fury* in America, "Certains esprits aiment les plaisirs faciles."[48]) It is mortifying to Americans to compare the reputation of Faulkner in his own country with that to be found in France at this period. Knowing very little about the man, the French judged him by his work, and accordingly placed him at or very near the top among writers in English in the twentieth century, almost from the beginning.

That Faulkner's reputation in France was so high, so early, was due to the work of Maurice Edgar Coindreau more than to any other single person. Beginning in 1931 a series of superb translations and critical articles by Coindreau led the way in introducing Faulkner to his audience in France. Important among these were his translation of *The Sound and the Fury*, which no serious study of the text of this work can afford to overlook, and his preface to this translation, which it has been the misfortune of American critics of the novel largely to ignore.

To Coindreau, Faulkner wrote early in 1937 that "After reading 'As I Lay Dying,'[49] in your translation, I am happy that you are considering undertaking S&F." To his most recent novel, *Absalom, Absalom!*, Faulkner had appended a short "Chronology" of dates and "Genealogy" of main characters, and he may have had something of the sort in mind when he offered to give Coindreau "any information you wish and I can about the book," adding "I wi[s]h you luck with it and I will be glad to draw up a chronology and genealogy and explanation, etc. if you need it."[50]

---

[48]M. E. Coindreau, preface to *Le bruit et la fureur*, p. 15.
[49]*Tandis que j'agonise,* Paris: Gallimard, 1934. With a preface by Valery Larbaud. Coindreau was working on this translation when he first met Faulkner, who inscribed for him his copy of the first edition (first state) of the novel: "William Faulkner | New York, N.Y. | 9 Nov 1931 | With gratitude to Dr Coindreau, the translator". (I am indebted to M. Coindreau for permitting me to use this inscription, seen May 1962.)
[50]This letter, dated 26 Feb. 1937, is reproduced in Plate II, *Princeton University Library Chronicle,* XVIII (Spring 1957).

Coindreau did not take up Faulkner on the offer of a chronology and genealogy, but for the explanation he journeyed to California — Faulkner at the time was serving one of his stretches in Hollywood, writing for the movies — in June 1937 and stayed a few days with him at his Beverly Hills duplex, 129 Ledoux Boulevard, while working on the translation. Although Faulkner would not reread the book, he cooperated wholeheartedly in the task of translation, freely discussing difficult passages with Coindreau, who was delighted, and somewhat astonished, at Faulkner's grasp of the details of the novel. Nearly eight years after its publication, the author's memory of the book was almost perfect. On only two occasions, according to Coindreau, did Faulkner's memory fail to produce the solution to the ambiguities in the novel which so often posed a problem for the translator.[51]

"Ambiguity is one aspect of Faulknerian obscurity," Coindreau has noted. As translator of Faulkner, one of his major problems was that "It is more difficult to be obscure in French than in English"; therefore, since the "English language lends itself readily to multiple interpretations," but the French language does not, it required constant care on his part to minimize the clarifying effect of the French tongue in passages of deliberate original ambiguity.[52] In accomplishing this, according to Coindreau, Faulkner's explanations of the ambiguities were of the greatest assistance.

The French translation of *The Sound and the Fury*, then, is — or should be — of concern to any careful critic of the novel for several reasons. The preface is of enduring interest. The French text, like any really good translation, is itself a kind of commen-

---

[51]Interviews with M. Coindreau, June 1957 and May 1962. In one of these interviews he told me that Faulkner very frequently referred him to another passage in the novel, for the solution to a problem in translating the text, instead of himself giving it; and that he often referred Coindreau to these passages by page number, and even located, still by memory, the passages upon the page. This is interesting, not because it reveals that Faulkner had a photographic memory of the book, but that he remembered it in its book form. Perhaps he had examined it closely when the novel was first published — he might well have done so, particularly if he saw no page proofs, since the editing of the first section had been so unsatisfactory. But it is more likely that the preparation of the copy for the abortive Random House edition, four years earlier, had given him so great a degree of familiarity with the book.

[52]M. E. Coindreau, "On Translating Faulkner," *Princeton University Library Chronicle,* XVIII (Spring 1957), 110. M. Coindreau makes the same point in the preface to his translation (p. 15): "Ayant eu le privilège d'entendre M. Faulkner me commenter lui-même les points les plus obscurs de son roman, je ne me suis dérobé devant aucun obstacle." Here too M. Coindreau apologizes for the fact that "la précision de la langue française m'a amené, malgré moi, à éclaircir le texte."

tary upon the original English, one which in this case is particularly valuable because of Faulkner's association with the process of translating it. Significant too is Faulkner's ready offer to provide Coindreau with the same sort of chronological-genealogical guide to the novel which had appeared in *Absalom, Absalom!*, and which he was a few years later to supply at some length for the readers of the Viking *Portable Faulkner*. But how many American critics have examined the text, or even read the preface, of *Le bruit et la fureur?* (This is to my knowledge the only occasion when Faulkner assisted in the translation of one of his works, but a number of the translations are undeservedly neglected by American critics, for they contain valuable and otherwise unavailable introductions.)

Just as Faulkner's interest in the Random House limited edition in the early 1930's revealed his continued interest in the typographical problems of the most effective way of handling Benjy's interior monologue, his reaction in 1945 to Malcolm Cowley's proposal to include an excerpt from *The Sound and the Fury* in a Faulkner anthology he was editing showed that he had not forgotten the idea he had broached to Coindreau in 1937 of providing for the novel some sort of reader's guide to its cast of characters. Cowley wanted to use part of the fourth section, and Faulkner sent him in October 1945 a kind of summary-commentary upon the main characters which in addition traced back the Compson family line through a number of generations not mentioned in the original book. In the Viking *Portable Faulkner*, where it is printed at the end of the volume at some remove from the excerpt from *The Sound and the Fury*, it makes a significant addition to the anthology's collection of high spots from Faulkner's fiction.

In the letter to Cowley which accompanied the piece, Faulkner apologized for any discrepancies with the novel it might contain, saying that he had no copy of *The Sound and the Fury*, but that if there were errors "which are too glaring to leave in and which you dont want to correct yourself," Cowley was to return the piece to him "with a note" — that is, presumably, with suggested corrections. Faulkner mentioned "chronology (various ages of people, etc)" and "the sum of money Quentin stole from her uncle Jason" as possibly inconsistent with the novel[53], and Cowley later described how he became aware of still others.[54]

---

[53]*Faulkner-Cowley File*, pp. 36-37.
[54]*Ibid.*, pp. 41-42.

When Cowley wrote him to point out some of these discrepancies, Faulkner defended them generally on several grounds. Clearly he was not much concerned by the sort of "errors" Cowley had found, particularly when they could be blamed upon the incomplete or faulty knowledge of a character in the work rather than upon its author. His most significant statement upon the subject had to do with the point of view of the entire Compson appendix, which he called a "genealogy". It had been written, he said, "to give a sort of bloodless bibliophile's point of view" of the characters; the author "was a sort of Garter King-at-Arms, heatless, not very moved, cleaning up 'Compson' before going on. . . ."[55] He did not, however, mention one of the most important reasons for the differences between the two works — the fact that already he had made additions to his original account of the Compson family. There are significant discrepancies between *The Sound and the Fury* and several other works which Faulkner wrote in the decade following the completion of the novel, including "That Evening Sun," "A Justice," and *Absalom, Absalom!;* the differences between the Compson appendix and *The Sound and the Fury* (and Faulkner's other fiction in which Compsons appear more than briefly) define the author's principle, to which he adhered with remarkable faithfulness throughout his career, of being consistently inconsistent — of never permitting past work to hinder his freedom in dealing with work at hand.

On November 2 1945 Cowley sent Faulkner carbon typescripts of the version of the excerpt from *The Sound and the Fury* which he planned to publish, and of the Compson appendix, which he had had retyped.[56] Faulkner soon returned the appendix — "with minor corrections that removed some, but not all, of the discrepancies" he had noted, Cowley recalled later, "if I remember correctly"[57]. On November 10 he again wrote Faulkner, suggesting

---

[55]*Ibid.*, p. 44. Cowley's note (p. 45) identifies the "Garter King-of-Arms" as the presiding officer of "the Heralds' College, or College of Arms, which rules on questions having to do with armorial bearings and pedigrees."

[56]*Ibid.*, p. 56. Among the Faulkner papers now at the University of Virginia are a 35 pp. carbon of the excerpt from *The Sound and the Fury*, which Cowley entitled "Dilsey," and two partial carbons of the Compson appendix, one of 12, the other of 22 pp. (*"Man Working"*, p. 230). The shorter version, which differs considerably from the published texts, appears to be from a typescript by Faulkner, probably of an early draft. The longer, which is complete except for p. 3, is apparently the one sent him by Cowley, for it appears to have been professionally typed, but it differs from the published versions in minor details.

[57]*Ibid.*, p. 56.

further changes in the appendix; Faulkner agreed to some, but
at one point demurred mildly that one inconsistency with the novel,
Quentin's climbing down a rain spout instead of a pear tree, was
not an error — "Could still be the Garter K/A, whose soul is one
inviolable literary cliché. He would insist on 'gutter'."[58]

Several months later Faulkner returned to the subject and gave
an additional excuse for the differences between these two Compson accounts when he wrote Cowley concerning a new project,
that of including the appendix in the proposed new Modern Library
edition of *The Sound and the Fury*. It had been suggested that
Faulkner write a new introduction for this edition. "I cant write
an introduction," Faulkner told Cowley. "I hope to hell Random
House cant find the other one I did" (that is, the one written
for the abortive Random House-Grabhorn edition). If the *Portable
Faulkner* Compson appendix were to be included, he said, he
"Would rather let the appendix stand with the inconsistencies,"
instead of rereading the novel and correcting the appendix. A
statement could be included, he went on to say (foreshadowing
the prefatory statement he was to supply thirteen years later for
The Mansion), that would explain his position,

> viz.: The inconsistencies in the appendix prove that to me the
> book is still alive after 15 years, and being still alive is growing,
> changing; the appendix was done at the same heat as the book,
> even though 15 years later, and so it is the book itself which is
> inconsistent: not the appendix. That is, at the age of 30 I did not
> know these people as at 45 I now do; that I was even wrong now
> and then in the very conclusions I drew from watching them, and
> the information in which I once believed.[59]

Though Faulkner's comments to Cowley about the Compson
appendix are obviously of great significance, it will not do to take
all his statements at face value. He clearly took the *Portable
Faulkner* seriously as an editorial project. But Cowley's enthusiasm
for the project did not prevent him from being more than a little

---

[58]*Ibid.*, p. 58.
[59]*Ibid.*, pp. 89-90. The prefatory note for *The Mansion* (New York: Random
House, 1959, p. [xi] explained any inconsistencies between it and the other
two volumes of the Snopes trilogy as being inevitable if his work was to have
life, since "the author has learned . . . more about the human heart and its
dilemma than he knew" before. Faulkner's attitude about the inconsistencies
within the trilogy, which help define the separate identities of its individual
novels, sheds additional light upon his willingness to consider the appendix
as related to *The Sound and the Fury* but not part of it.

condescending toward Faulkner at the time, and Faulkner was in turn a little defensive and cagey, and by no means above pulling Cowley's leg a little. On the whole it seems safe to say that Faulkner was intrigued at the notion of writing something that would serve to introduce an excerpt from *The Sound and the Fury* to readers of the anthology; that in the writing of it, it became more an afterword upon the Compson family than an introduction to the excerpt; that he was quite aware that his vision of the novel's characters had changed since he first wrote it; that he refused on principle to familiarize himself again with the novel and eliminate or even minimize the discrepancies between it and the appendix; and probably that he expected anyone who read the appendix (at least in conjunction with the novel) to be aware of the differences between two such works, written years apart, and especially to be aware of differences in point of view. But a good many critics who have dealt with *The Sound and the Fury* since the publication of the appendix have failed to make any real distinction between them. (An exception might be made for Faulkner's French critics; since the novel has never been published there with the appendix attached to it, there have been almost none of the critical *faux pas* committed in France, like the sentimentalization of the character of Luster, which certain American critics appear to owe to reading the appendix more closely than the novel.)

The inclusion of the Compson appendix in the new Modern Library edition of *The Sound and the Fury* adds legitimate textual confusion to the spurious critical issue of the discrepancies between the two works, for the Modern Library text of the appendix differs from that which had appeared in the *Portable Faulkner*. Faulkner had written Cowley early in 1946 to send Random House a copy of the appendix to include in the new Modern Library volume.[60] Cowley, instead, sent a copy to Faulkner, and wrote to Robert Linscott at Random House that he had done so. He cautioned Linscott about the discrepancies—Faulkner's "memory was faulty at two or three points," he noted, and went on to say that he was going to lend Faulkner his own copy of *The Sound and the Fury* "and tell him that he has to do some rewriting."[61]

---

[60]*Ibid.*, p. 85.
[61]*Ibid.*, p. 86.

Commenting later on the differences between the two published versions of the appendix, Cowley stated that "Faulkner had worked a little more" on the Modern Library version; "he had accepted some of my emendations, rejected others, and revised his entry on Jason Compson. He had not attempted, however, to resolve the several discrepancies between the appendix and the earlier text of the novel."[62] It is not clear, however, that the differences between the two published texts are accounted for by authorial revision *after* Cowley had had retyped, and had edited, the original version, which seems to have disappeared. The typescript which Cowley sent Faulkner may have been closer to the original, unedited text than that which was published in the *Portable Faulkner*, and may in turn have been sent on by Faulkner to Random House with little or no further revision. Lacking further evidence we can only speculate, but it is clear that the version in the Modern Library contained fewer of Cowley's editorial changes than did the version in the *Portable Faulkner*, and that we badly need a better published text of the appendix, as close as possible to the one that Faulkner wrote.

In the *Portable Faulkner* the Compson appendix appeared at the end of the volume and separated by other stories from the excerpt which Cowley had included from *The Sound and the Fury*. In the 1946 Modern Library edition of the novel, however, the appendix was printed at the beginning; being made, in effect, to serve the function of the new introduction which Faulkner had refused to write for it. The title-page of the volume claims for it *"A NEW APPENDIX AS A FOREWORD BY THE AUTHOR."* The text of this edition is thus off to a very poor start, spoiling the effect of the novel's original beginning with Benjy's monologue, and failing to explain that this "Foreword" had originally been written for inclusion in an anthology, not an edition of the novel. Unwary readers found themselves presented with what appears to be a five-part novel, the first part of which relieves them of the burdens which the second part was originally designed to impose upon them in the way of careful and creative reading.

The 1946 Modern Library text suffers from more than just the presence of this Appendix-as-Foreword. Collation with the 1929 edition reveals the presence of no authorial revision or correction, and though a few minor corrections of errors and incon-

---

[62]*Ibid.*, p. 89.

sistencies in the original were made,[63] a great many new printer's errors were committed. As Table C reveals, most of them are in themselves unimportant, but a few affect substantively the meaning of the passages in which they occur, and when added to the lesser errors of the original edition, the total effect is demonstrably unfortunate.

Not listed in the table are a number of minor editorial changes, like *a while* for *awhile* and *any more* for *anymore*, which are

TABLE C

ERRORS IN THE MODERN LIBRARY *The Sound and the Fury*

Modern Library		Cape and Smith	Modern Library		Cape and Smith
23.19	went	went back	154.2	*oh*	*Oh*
25.18	wonder.	wonder	155.26	*and mud*	*the mud*
38.16	up on	up	158.30	got a	a
41.30	It was	I was	161.1	curb	curb,
46.28	ain't	aint	175.33	window	windows
47.2	back	black	193.25	*I wouldnt have*	I wouldnt have
47.4	Mr.	Mr	194.29	right.	right
52.24	*Frony,*	*Frony*	199.7	her	her.
57.4	*nobody*	*aint nobody*	202.5	her;	her,
59.24	Cad	Caddy	227.29	trying	tr-trying
59.27	*said Benjy*	*said, Benjy*	228.15	Rogers."	Rogers'."
63.19	door	door.	229.12	can	cant
63.34	whispered	whispered.	270.21	fom	fum
66.25	whispered	whispered.	272.24	from	fum
68.34	ain't	aint	273.26	ask	act
69.18	lost	lost."	281.1	CHILL.	CHILL,
71.31	Don't	Dont	285.2	less	less,
74.22	can't	cant	285.29	H'h	Hah
82.6	Hush.'	Hush."	286.11	breadboard	bread board
99.15	flatiron	flat-iron	289.2	what	whar
109.9	that it would	that would	289.4	last	Last
123.33	to	too	291.6	'lawd	Lawd
124.18	that breathed	*that breathed*	292.16	you	yo
125.26	that	than	294.24	yo	you
127.33	hit off	hit it off	297.18	have	yet have
130.24	Massachusetts	in Massachusetts	298.18	other	the other
134.34	razor,	razor	300.15	ready—	read—
144.30	stage	stage.	300.26	and	on and
145.8	standing	just standing	317.29	don't	dont
145.33	took	took up	321.30	nor	nor of
146.12	dirty-dress	dirty dress	327.4	your eye	your
147.15	horse	white horse	327.5	an eye	a human eye
147.25	Feetsoles	Feet soles	331.31	dont	done
149.14	facade	façade	336.6	They	Then

[63]The following errors listed in Table A were corrected in the Modern Library edition: 33.20, 75.5, 84.5, 125.12, 168.1, 216.14, 240.29, 273.4, 324.2, 357.14, 357.17, and 369.13.

made inconsistently, and where the first edition was likewise inconsistent. Also not listed are the numerous places where the Modern Library edition omitted the spaces which in the original, in Quentin's section, served as a kind of punctuation. Again, there is sufficient inconsistency in the way the matter is handled in the original to make it appear not worthwhile to note the variations in the Modern Library edition.

The 1946 Modern Library text of *The Sound and the Fury* was many times reprinted during the next twenty years, both in the original double volume with *As I Lay Dying* and separately, in the cheaper format of the Modern Library Paperback and Vintage imprints. Two new American editions in the 1950's gave even wider circulation to this negligible text[64] before the original 1929 edition was finally reissued by Random House in 1966. Reproduced by photo-offset from a copy of the first printing of the novel, the text of this reissue was made available as a cloth-bound trade book under the Random House imprint, and as a Modern Library book which also included the Compson appendix, this time more appropriately placed at the end of the volume. (Its text is reset and a few minor editorial changes are made.)

The Sound and the Fury was a critical success when it was first published and its author was virtually unknown, and since that time its reputation has grown, with its author's, until perhaps no American novel of this century is esteemed more highly throughout the world. But despite the large, and increasing, body of critical work upon it that has appeared, it is obvious that as yet we have hardly seen a beginning to the really intensive investigation of this difficult and demanding, but rich and rewarding book. Its sources, its imagery, its relationship with other Faulkner works, perhaps even such basic elements as its structure and the function of its three interior monologues all demand further study, and any general studies of Faulkner's mind and art must pay it especial attention because of the unique place it had in his development and retained in his affections.

But it is obvious too that the close readings which *The Sound and the Fury* deserves, and will receive, require as good a text as it is possible to publish. Faulkner's careful preservation of his original manuscript and typescript will make it possible, I do not

---

[64]That is, the *Faulkner Reader* and Signet editions. (See fn. 1.)

doubt, to produce an edition of the novel significantly closer to his intention than any yet published. And eventually we should have, in addition to a "definitive" text of the novel, based on the typescript, an edition of the manuscript itself, which Faulkner revised and expanded in so many ways when he typed it.[65] But we must mourn the opportunity that was lost, during the depression, of bringing out under the author's supervision an edition both textually and typographically worthy of this ambitious and moving novel, which Faulkner so often referred to as the one closest to his heart, of all he wrote.

---

[65]We need too, of course, a better text of the Compson appendix, one based upon a study of all the surviving typescripts of the work, which will eliminate the various editorial changes made to minimize its "discrepancies" with the novel.

Walter Brylowski

From "The Dark Vision: Myth in *The Sound and the Fury*"

Faulkner criticism, even from the time regarded by his present critics as the dark ages of his fame, has shown an awareness of the quality of myth in his writings. Perhaps this awareness has been stimulated by a renewed attention to the study of myth, which began at about the same time that criticism became aware of Faulkner. While the two areas of study have been developed in parallel periods, they have met only casually. "Myth" appears in many studies of Faulkner, but the meaning of the word is often unclear. At times it may be used to signify a fiction embraced by a culture as a representation of some essential truth of exis-tence, a definition central to the work of the Cambridge School of myth-ritual scholars. Again, it might be used in a more casual sense to denote fictions compounded in the form of a saga and thus serve as a label for the Yoknapatawpha works. Or "myth" might be determined from context to import some large world

From chapter one, "Faulkner's Mythology," and chapter three, "The Dark Vision," of *Faulkner's Olympian Laugh,* by Walter Brylowski, Detroit: Wayne State University Press, 1968. Reprinted by permission of the Wayne State University Press.

view for which the critic intends to supply a schematized explanation. In any case, there is usually too much taken for granted in the use of the term with much ambiguity resulting. The word "myth" has come to have sonorous overtones in the modern critical vocabulary and, due to a multitude of possible meanings, has become, like the bearded patriarch, a symbol evoking unexamined respect. It is not my purpose to destroy that respect, but to examine the basis for it and perhaps thereby to enhance its dignity.

To do this, it will be necessary to distinguish between various levels of myth apparent in Faulkner's work. The first and simplest level of myth is that of allusion and analogy. As allusion, the references to classical myths in the earlier work might most kindly be termed naive decoration. Faulkner, however, quickly abandons his excessive attraction to this rhetorical embroidery and by the time of *The Sound and the Fury* the pose of classicism is transferred from the implied author to a character, Mr. Compson, where it serves the function of accenting a debilitating divorcement from action. However, the references to classical myths used in a simple analogical manner do not suffer the same fate. In the early period, before *The Sound and the Fury*, these are found largely as compressed similes, adjectives applied to characters with the facility of stock epithets. These undergo a functional transformation as Faulkner's use of myth becomes thematic, and, as in *Absalom, Absalom!*, become integrated with the "myth" in the sense of plot. It is on this level that we might include many of Faulkner's uses of the Christian myth.

What I would term the second level of myth to be found in his works is to be distinguished from the first level in degree rather than in kind, for here too myth functions as analogy. But on this level, myth is not to be considered as a trope integrated with the plot; instead, it *is* plot. Thus, though there are many images which strike analogies between Joe Christmas and Christ, it is the larger mythic pattern of the scapegoat which governs the action and which includes both Christ and Joe Christmas. Myth and theme here are inseparable; myth arises from theme and informs theme. Within the body of Faulkner's work, two such archetypal patterns of mythic action occur: the casting out of the scapegoat and the initiation of the youth.

On the third level of myth there is a sharp distinction in kind. Here we pass from the rhetoric of the first level and the *mythos* of the second level to an examination of the epistemology of the actors and even to a consideration of that of the author. Here

I shall use the term "mythic mode of thought" derived from Cassirer's attempt to achieve a philosophic definition of myth as symbolic form:

> To seek a "form" of mythical consciousness in this sense, means to inquire neither after its ultimate metaphysical causes nor after its psychological, historical or social causes: it is solely to seek the unity of the spiritual *principle* by which all its particular configurations, with all their vast empirical diversity, appear to be governed. . . . a critical phenomenology of the mythical consciousness . . . will seek to apprehend the subject of the cultural process, the human spirit, solely in its pure actuality and diverse configurations, whose immanent norms it will strive to ascertain.[1]

Cassirer's discussion examines the consciousness of the object as "the product of a formative operation effected by the basic instrumentality of consciousness, by intuition and pure thought" (p. 29), and differentiates between this consciousness as it appears in mythical thought and as it appears in theoretical-scientific or rational-empiric thought. It will be my object to examine the epistemology of some of Faulkner's characters and to demonstrate that their configurations of reality which frustrate analysis attempted in terms of the rational-empiric mode of thought, can be explained more satisfactorily in terms of the mythic mode.

When we begin to consider the nature of some of Faulkner's own thoughts as evidenced by his novels, we raise the problem of the relation of myth to art. Here again there is a problem about the meaning of "myth." Richard Chase, limiting the meaning of "myth" to a formulated story, then equates all myth with art. This is to obscure the problem, for there is the vast area of mythic thought, of myth formation to be considered. When I speak of the mythic mode of thought, I shall mean the spiritual activity of the individual seeking to create a configuration of reality, an activity that is determined by laws other than the rational-empiric, which have received their most coherent analysis in Cassirer's study. This much will suffice for the characters of the novels. However, when we speak of the artist we must remember that in the creation of his work he has already divorced himself from the primary quality of myth, the immediacy with which the mythic mode seizes upon the essential unity of the subject-object relation.

---

[1]Ernst Cassirer, *The Philosophy of Symbolic Forms,* translated by Ralph Manheim, New Haven: Yale University Press, 1955, vol. II, *Mythical Thought,* pp. 11-12, 13.

The artist's world of the *logos* acknowledges at once a removal into the area of pure forms where this primary unity does not exist.

It is possible, therefore, for a character within a novel to be presented as operating within the mythic mode, a character whose epistemology is governed by the laws of myth formation; but when we speak of the artist's work as myth we are already approaching another realm. The mythic mode of thought, governed by the immediacy and unity of the subject-object relation, is expressed in action. The participant in ritual action *becomes* the subject of his actions. The myth that arises *after* the ritual already admits of the distance between the subject and object. So long as the myth commands complete belief it remains in the area of the mythic mode. However, once this belief disappears, we have a fiction, a residue which now has a new being in the rational-empiric world. The writer of fiction is, then, not a creator of myth. We must grant him the ability to recognize the subject-object distance, the ability to resist the equation of his work with what we call empiric reality. To equate fiction with myth does credit to neither. I believe it *is* possible, however, to speak of the degree to which fiction can approximate the quality of myth. Here we may dignify both myth and the writer of fiction. The artist's recognition of the force of myth in man's spiritual activity and his desire — even necessity — to use this as a tool wherewith to express his own intuitions constitutes a valid area of study.

The artist's intuitions are frequently beyond the ability of language used in its rational-empiric fashion to express, yet the artist must find his expression. "*Intuitive activity possesses intuitions to the extent that it expresses them.*"[2] Several critics have remarked the dissatisfaction Faulkner expresses in his early novels with "talk, talk talk," and I believe it is his felt need to discover a mode of communication which carries an aura of meaning beyond the bounds of what might be recognized as a scientifically rational mode of knowledge that leads him to employ the perceptions of irrational characters, characters whose "truth" is a configuration of the mythic mode of thought. The discovery of this as a tool of his art marks the beginning of that series of books labeled the great middle period.

As Faulkner's thinking centers around an examination of the nature of evil, the experiments in form and structure become

---

[2]Benedetto Croce, *Aesthetic,* transl. Douglas Ainslie, London: Macmillan, 1909, p. 13.

almost dominant. The function of his mythic analogues becomes an exploration of evil beyond the bounds of morality. It is a mode allowing him to treat in narrative form his vision of a world permeated with evil and yet to balance this with his faith that evil will, in the long run, consume itself while the "verities" — courage, honor, love — will maintain their static nobility and allow man to "endure." It is possible to trace a progression through Faulkner's works of his coming to grips with the problem of evil in terms of this mythic mode of thought. There is ample evidence in the early novels that he was well acquainted with the residual myths of the classical period, but there is a little evidence that he had penetrated to the significance that informed them before they had lost their true mythic meaning. There is later evidence that Faulkner was acquainted with the work of the anthropologists in the area of myth studies and, in the middle period, his work begins to employ techniques which result in a movement toward the true force represented by myth. In the later period, forecast by *The Unvanquished* and covering the novels from *Go Down, Moses* to *A Fable*, his work reflects the evolution of the mythic consciousness to the mythical-religious consciousness, a movement which reveals his own intellectual resolution of the problem of evil through transcendence. . . .

．　．　．

Carvel Collins cites four sketches that provide material later reworked in *The Sound and the Fury*, the most obvious being "in 'The Kingdom of God' the cornflower blue eyes of the idiot, his broken narcissus, his bellowing, and his silent departure from the final furious scene [which] anticipate the extended and effective treatment of Benjy."[3] There is also in *Mosquitoes* the image already noted of the steward David huddled over the soiled slipper which becomes part of Benjy's characterization. Benjy's perception of Caddy, "Caddy smelled like trees" (p. 5), has also been long in the works. In *Soldiers' Pay* it appears as the allusive image of the hamadryad and in the equation of trees and young virginal girls;[4] in *Mosquitoes*, Talliaferro is aware of "the clean young odor" of Patricia, "like that of young trees."[5] The history of this image suggests that long before *The Sound and the Fury*

[3]Collins, ed. *William Faulkner: New Orleans Sketches.* New Brunswick: Rutgers University Press, 1958, pp. 27-29.
[4]*Soldiers' Pay,* New York: Boni and Liveright, 1926, pp. 77, 292.
[5]*Mosquitoes,* New York: Boni and Liveright, 1927, p. 21.

Faulkner's imagination had fixed upon an equation between virginity and straight, slim trees, an image further extended to include the odor of each as the identifying principle, the sense of smell being labeled by Faulkner as "one of my sharper senses."[6] The image originally taken from classical mythology has grown into a complicated focal image moving toward the biblical realm of Eden, containing within itself an emotional center for a new and more mature examination of the problem of evil. Whereas the early novels focused upon a problem of evil that was merely social and called forth a rather shallow evaluation, the novels of the middle period are centered on a more metaphysical concept of evil, essentially mythic in that it is emotionally centered and given formulation through the narrative mode rather than centered in any objective quest for knowledge through an explicitly philosophical mode. The glib handling of a misguided society operating in terms of an inadequate value system with the author conspicuously present as the representative of a norm of values is forsaken for a direct presentation of a personal, emotional vision of man's estate.

In his later comments on the novel, Faulkner constantly returned to the image of Caddy as a child climbing the tree to look in the window:

> . . . the explanation of that whole book is in that. It began with the picture of the little girl's muddy drawers, climbing that tree to look in the parlor window with her brothers that didn't have the courage to climb the tree waiting to see what she saw. And I tried first to tell it with one brother, and that wasn't enough. That was Section One. I tried with another brother, and that wasn't enough. That was Section Two. I tried the third brother, because Caddy was still to me too beautiful and too moving to reduce her to telling what was going on, that it would be more passionate to see her through somebody else's eyes, I thought. And that failed and I tried myself — the fourth section — to tell what happened, and I still failed.[7]

When questioned again about this "impression," Faulkner elaborated his explanation:

> Well, impression is the wrong word. It's more an image, a very moving image to me was of the children. 'Course, we didn't know

---

[6]Frederick L. Gwynn and Joseph L. Blotner, eds. *Faulkner in the University,* Charlottesville: University of Virginia Press, 1959, p. 253.
[7]*Ibid.,* p. 1.

at that time that one was an idiot, but they were three boys, one
was a girl and the girl was the only one that was brave enough to
climb that tree to look in the forbidden window to see what was
going on. And that's what the book — and it took the rest of the
four hundred pages to explain why she was brave enough to climb
the tree to look in the window. It was an image, a picture to me, a
very moving one, which was symbolized by the muddy bottom of
her drawers as her brothers looked up into the apple tree that she
had climbed to look in the window. And the symbolism of the
muddy bottom of the drawers became the lost Caddy. . . .[8]

The central image, as it has been designated by Faulkner,
reveals the mythic approach to the problem of evil. The satiric
pose of the first two novels is explicitly brushed aside in a comment before the Department of Psychiatry at the University of
Virginia:

. . . I think the writer is not really interested in bettering man's
condition. He really doesn't care a damn about man's condition.
He's interested in all man's behavior with no judgment whatever.
That it's motion, it's life, the only alternative is nothingness, death.
And so to the writer, anything man does is fine because it's motion.
. . . Maybe the writer has no concept of morality at all, only an
integrity to hold always to what he believes to be the facts and
truths of human behavior, not moral standards at all.[9]

But while abjuring "moral standards," it is evident that his
avowed objectivity (expressed as hindsight and certainly not
including the first two novels) does not extend itself to dismiss
the abstract problem of evil in conflict with good, or more specifically, the problem of sustaining optimistic faith in man's ability
to subscribe to ideals or "verities" in the immediate and almost
overwhelming presence of physical and moral decay. The problem
of sustaining such a faith is more a problem for Faulkner, the
artist and the man, than for any of his characters, and it is a
struggle that informs his work from this point on.

The image of Caddy suggests the inevitability of loss of innocence through the muddied drawers, but Faulkner's emphasis in
reviewing the novel is on the courage — one of his "verities" —
embodied in the climb to look in the "forbidden window" upon
the presence of death. When Dilsey comes out to put an end to

---

[8]*Ibid.*, p. 31.
[9]*Ibid.*, p. 267.

the scene it is " 'You, Satan.' Dilsey said. 'Come down from there' " (p. 54). It would seem that for Faulkner, Caddy in this crucial scene shares a role similar to Milton's Satan in the Romantics' eyes — the courage of defiance.

From Faulkner's comments it would appear that *The Sound and the Fury* was intended to be Caddy's story and was probably to be dominated by the image of Eden and the courage to claim forbidden knowledge. This comes to focus in his later comments in Virginia where even the tree Caddy climbed becomes specifically an apple tree, that in the novel is mentioned only in Quentin's musings on his sister. The oblique narrative method intended to exempt her from any involvement in the telling results, however, in a much larger story with her moving out of the reader's range of vision almost entirely. The image which ostensibly gave impetus to the story does not dominate it. The equation of virgin with tree or smell of trees does not carry with it any moral value of good: the drawers are muddied as a foreshadowing of what is for Faulkner the inevitable *natural* fallen state. Caddy's courage in climbing the tree for forbidden knowledge is the same courage which allows her to accept life and the forbidden knowledge of sex. This is contrasted to the neurotic rejection of sex by Quentin who symbolically drops the knife held at Caddy's throat after she has refused to put her hand on it, an act that would have constituted a symbolic consummation of incest. Earlier, employing another phallic symbol, Quentin rejects the gun offered him by Dalton Ames after Ames has demonstrated its effectiveness. Quentin's mind wanders over the pressures of sex which he cannot cope with in any natural manner:

> . . . Versh told me about a man mutilated himself. He went into the woods and did it with a razor, sitting in a ditch. A broken razor flinging them backward over his shoulder the same motion complete the jerked skein of blood backward not looping. But that's not it. It's not not having them. It's never to have had them then I could say O That That's Chinese I dont know Chinese. And Father said it's because you are a virgin: dont you see? Women are never virgins. Purity is a negative state and therefore contrary to nature. It's nature is hurting you not Caddy and I said That's just words and he said So is virginity and I said you dont know. . . . [p. 143]

Of the other two brothers, one is a gelding and the other resorts to sex without love. But if sex and a kind of Shavian life force were to be the center of values, Caddy's daughter Quentin would have to share equally with her mother the honor of courage. However, there is no apple tree for Quentin: her prosaic promiscuous rendezvous are via the pear tree. The reader almost feels cheated when Quentin, who has become a fully realized character, triumphs over Jason but is immediately and forever dismissed by Faulkner who continues to cling to Caddy, even fabricating her continued existence among the Nazis in his later comments on the characters of the novel in the appendix provided for *The Portable Faulkner*.

If morality in terms of sex does not provide the rationale of evil, where does it lie? Its center is in the absence of Christian love, *agape*, and the novel is successful not in its exploitation of the fall through knowledge, but in its unremitting examination of various eccentricities which throw the ego in upon itself to the exclusion of any ability to love. Once Caddy, who had this ability to love, is exiled, the scene is a waste land of activity signifying nothing, until the final chapter when Dilsey's pilgrimage to the church with Frony, Luster, and Benjy is offered as an action of endurance. The novel ends with Jason restoring the world of the idiot "each in its ordered place," and we are left with the sense that the "order" is the stasis and sterility of the waste land.

The informing myth of the novel is not, then, that of the fall but of the god of love crucified. Its theme is an examination of an Emersonian evil: the absence of good. It is on the second level of myth, as theme, the total integration with plot, that this is most apparent, and here the allusions are all to the Christian myth of crucifixion and resurrection. But before proceeding to this, I might cite the few allusions on the first level of myth. Shreve alludes to Mrs. Bland as a Semiramis (p. 125) and Quentin, brooding upon Caddy's sexual experiences with Dalton Ames, alludes to the swine of Euboeleus (p. 184), the mythical swineherd who saw the rape of Persephone on the way to the underworld and passed the information on to the searching Demeter. Karl Zink, writing of "Faulkner's Garden: Woman and the Immemorial Earth," generalizes about Faulkner's pregnant women:

> Despite the fact that so many of these women are unmarried, they are good women; they have an integrity that conventionally respectable women in the novels consistently do not have. These women, more than their men, are akin to the "fecund" earth, like the earth itself potential sources for renewal and development, for physical continuity within the continuous process of Nature.[10]

[10]*Modern Fiction Studies,* II (Autumn 1956), p. 143.

In speaking of Eula Varner, Zink advances the image of Persephone. "Only with Eula's return, like Persephone, the following spring, does the dessicated land know release and respond normally to the plow" (p. 141). Although he does not cite the Euboeleus allusion in connection with Caddy, the image functions in much the same way, reinforcing the sterility of the Compson world when Caddy's fruitful promiscuity relegates her to the "underworld" of Mrs. Compson. Unlike Eula, she does not return bringing with her the fructifying spring.

Shreve, trying to explain why Quentin began the fight with Gerald Bland which has resulted in his thorough beating, brings in an allusion to Leda and the swan (pp. 206-07). And in the amazing compression of the last few pages of his monologue, as he is preparing ritually for his death by drowning, Quentin's mind wanders over images of water which associate with sleep, the sleep of death he is seeking. Going from his room to the bathroom becomes associated with the child's journey for a late night drink, the fixtures *"less than Moses rod"* (p. 216). There is one passing allusion to Cupid, "the blind immortal boy" (p. 217) in association with Uncle Maury, the philanderer.

On the second level, the integration of the Christian myth demonstrates more of the continuity of imagery from the earlier novels with a radical shift in emphasis. The hopeful image of the resurrection loosely tacked on the end of *Soldiers' Pay* and glibly dropped throughout *Mosquitoes* in relation to the Gordon-Israfel character is now superimposed on the total action of the novel through a structural device which forces it to carry a great burden of meaning. What began in the early novels as a debate between a cloddish society and a cocky, sophomoric young man has become a dialogue between a highly verbal, aggressive awareness of evil and a mute, indomitable, and perhaps sentimental faith in "verities." The "mute" participant in this dialogue makes itself known largely through the structure of the novel until in the last section, the attempt by Faulkner himself to tell the story, Dilsey is brought forward as an almost sentimental antidote to the large doses of corruption and decay which have made up the major part of the story. It is Faulkner's strength as an artist that he communicates evil well — "it's easier to conceive of evil than of good . . . easier to make believable, credible, than good"[11] — and his weakness that in portraying the struggle between good and evil, the powers

---

[11]*Faulkner in the University*, p. 5.

of light appear to have been grossly mismatched. His vision of evil lies completely within the rational-empiric realm. When he attempts to communicate his intuition of the sustaining verities, he seems to be aware of the danger of falling off into sentimentality as in the portrayal of Dilsey. I believe it is the need to communicate the positive element of his vision by some means other than direct statement or characterization that leads to his highly experimental forms that suggest more obliquely, that communicate indirectly the positive pole of his vision as a counterbalance to the direct dramatic presentation of evil.

The structural device of the dates of the three parts focused around Easter seems to suggest the lost soul (Benjy) in hell on Saturday, the killing of the god of love (through Jason's characterization) on Friday, and the resurrection with its *potential* hope on Sunday. This antithesis between a realistic portrayal of moral and social corruption and the inclusion of hopeful idealistic elements which are so vague and amorphous that they must be suggested by structural juxtaposition or by allusion to the myths which embody man's greatest hopes, constitutes the most unifying element in Faulkner's work. His oft-repeated sense of failure in *The Sound and the Fury* might have been due to the shift from the Eden myth to the killing of the god of love, but this failure can easily be dismissed as a product of the intentional fallacy and not justified by the work. What cannot be dismissed, however, is the mistake in the choice of the analogue which calls for a thoroughly triumphant denouement which Faulkner is obviously unable to accept. The myth of the resurrection is too strong and too concrete in its connotations for his faith, which at this point in his intellectual history must content itself with vague abstractions that cannot triumph over the vital and concrete expressions of evil.

The Christian myth is used explicitly in the text as a norm for the values of love missing from the lives of the characters. Mrs. Compson, in her maudlin egocentricity, complains, " 'Nobody knows how I dread Christmas. Nobody knows' " (p. 7). And when, in the last section, she explains to Jason about letting the servants go to special Easter services, her whining justification is: " 'I know it's my fault. . . . I know you blame me.' 'For what?' Jason said. 'You never resurrected Christ, did you?' " (p. 348). Mrs. Compson, one of Faulkner's most brilliantly realized characters, stands at the core of the novel as she stands at the core of the family, the decay and disintegration of the Compsons effected largely by her failure — that passes through Quentin's mind as: *"My little sister had no. If I could say Mother. Mother"* (p. 117) and *". . . if I'd just had a mother so I could say Mother Mother"* (p. 213).

The similarities between Mrs. Compson and her son Jason are made explicit by her constant avowals that he is her only true child, a true Bascomb. On Good Friday, perhaps his most symbolic action is dropping the free passes for the tent show into the fire as Luster watches, a dramatic indication of the absence of human feeling. His monologue is punctuated by the repetitious use of *hell* as the only mythic reference, and in view of the novel's tight structure it must be viewed as having that significance.

Jason's characterization, however, is most interesting in another respect. Here we find Faulkner's first attempt at a dramatic presentation of the solution to the problem of evil. For those who suffer under evil, endurance is the only answer: the solution is that evil will create its own destruction. (Later Faulkner modifies this position in accordance with a more positive view of the power of man's spirit.) In Jason we find this pattern offered for the first time. The evil which is found in the egocentricity of the Bascombs (and against which the Compson blood has no defense to offer) finally outwits itself. Jason, whose only symbol of success is money (his name designates the pursuit of the golden, and for fleece Faulkner provides the speculation in cotton) is outmaneuvered in his cotton speculations and by the niece from whom he has been stealing money over the years. Uncle Job, the Negro worker at the store, sums up the point:

> "I wont try to fool you," he says. "You too smart fer me. Yes, suh," he says, looking busy as hell, putting five or six little packages into the wagon, "You's too smart fer me. Aint a man in dis town kin keep up wid you fer smartness. You fools a man whut so smart he cant even keep up wid hisself," he says, getting in the wagon and unwrapping the reins.
> "Who's that?" I says.
> "Dat's Mr Jason Compson," he says. [pp. 311-12]

For Faulkner there is no "just retribution" for evil which would imply an abstract moral scheme; there is only the irony of events. With Jason and with Flem Snopes, the actions they have set in motion merely turn back on them. With Popeye, it is the irony of happenstance. Nor do these setbacks result in the triumph of any abstract "good." It is merely man in motion, which for

Faulkner is the meaning of life: "That it's motion, it's life, the
only alternative is nothingness, death."

The greatest concentration of allusions to myths is found in
Quentin's monologue, reinforcing the nature of his perception of
reality which I should like to examine as the mythic mode. Carvel
Collins has suggested that the three brothers might be studied
as Faulkner's conscious fragmentation of the mind according to
Freud's theory.[12] I too should like to advance a scheme of sorts,
not far removed from Professor Collins' Freudian analysis but in
terms of Cassirer's analysis of the mythic mode.[13] Benjy's monologue may be viewed as a pre-mythic apprehension of the world,
Quentin's as an example of the mythic configuration of the world,
and Jason's as an example of the rational empirical mode.

Benjy's monologue does not reveal any coherent configuration of
reality. His perceptions are chaotic, disoriented in any time-space
relationship; his world remains a chaos of impressions.[14] At the
other extreme, Jason's configuration of the world is best characterized by Faulkner's later comments in his appendix: "The first
sane Compson since before Culloden and (a childless bachelor)
hence the last. Logical rational contained and even a philosopher
in the old stoic tradition . . ." (p. 420). It remains to examine
Quentin's mode of perception as the intermediary stage in this
epistemological progression.

"It is one of the first essential insights of critical philosophy,"
says Cassirer,

> that objects are not "given" to consciousness in a rigid, finished
> state, in their naked "as suchness," but that the relation of repre-
> sentation to object presupposes an independent, spontaneous act
> of consciousness. The object does not exist prior to and outside of

[12]In "The Interior Monologues of *The Sound and the Fury*" (p. 63 in this
collection).
[13]Susanne K. Langer has pointed out the closeness of Cassirer's theory of
mind to Freud's. But Cassirer refused to explore the "fund of corroborative
evidence" offered by the field of "dynamic psychology" because he felt that
Freud considered all cultural achievements to be mere by-products of the
libido; "whereas to him they were the consummation of a spiritual process
which merely took its rise from the blind excitement of the animal 'libido,'
but received its importance and meanings from the phenomena of awareness
and creativity, the envisagement, reason, and cognition it produced." "On
Cassirer's Theory of Language and Myth," *The Philosophy of Ernst Cassirer*,
ed. P. A. Schilpp, Evanston, Illinois: Library of Living Philosophers, 1949,
p. 395.
[14]Philip Wheelwright mentions Benjy in this manner in *The Burning Foun-
tain*, Bloomington: Indiana University Press, 1954, p. 160.

synthetic unity but is constituted only by this synthetic unity. . . .
The *Philosophy of Symbolic Forms* . . . seeks the categories of the
consciousness of objects in the theoretical, intellectual sphere, and
starts from the assumption that such categories must be at work
wherever a cosmos, a characteristic and typical world view, takes
form out of the chaos of impressions. All such world views are
made possible only by specific acts of objectivization, in which mere
impressions are reworked into specific, formed representations.[15]

It is this "cosmos" that is missing from the world view of Benjy.
A synthetic unity is given the disordered impressions by the reader
in terms of his later knowledge of these events, but taken alone
Benjy's section would remain largely unintelligible to the reader.
It is the reader who must perform the act of objectivization and
rework the material into a formed representation.

It is Cassirer's methodology in his study of the mythical consciousness to work backward through the strata of the consciousness of the object preceding the "theoretical object-consciousness
of our experience" to determine the possible variants "the *direction*
and *means* of this process of objectivization" may have. It is
here that he makes the distinction between the mythic mode and
the scientific-empiric mode. Empirical reality, he says, is distinguished from the mere world of representation or imagination
in that "the permanent is more and more clearly differentiated
from the fluid, the constant from the variable." Sense impressions
gain the status of determinate objective existence only if they can
be confirmed by experience as a whole, and this constant testing of
experience results in the changes in that which we call objective
reality (p. 31).

The aim of this scientific-empiric mode of thought is to achieve
a universal synthesis; but to achieve this order pre-supposes a
corresponding analysis. "Where the sensory world view sees only a
peaceable coexistence, . . . empirical-theoretical thinking finds an
interpenetration, a complex of 'conditions.' " The sensory world
view is content to establish the mere "what" of the given, whereas
the scientific-empiric mode transforms the "what" into "because"
and replaces the mere coexistence of the contents of apprehension
in space and time with an ideal dependency. Since this ideal
dependency is not a factor of sensory perception, its prominence
tends to displace the sensory perception from the center of objectivity. "The objective significance of an element of experience

---

[15]*The Philosophy of Symbolic Forms*, vol. II, p. 29.

depends no longer on the sensuous force with which it individually strikes consciousness, but on the clarity with which the form, the law of the whole, is expressed and reflected in it" (pp. 32-4). This process of analysis and synthesis by which theoretical knowledge arrives at a concept of objectivity involves the constant differentiation between the "accidental" and the "essential."

> Myth too lives in a world of pure forms which it looks upon as thoroughly objective . . . . But its relation to this world discloses no sign of that decisive "crisis" with which empirical and conceptual knowledge begin. Its contents, to be sure, are given in an objective form, as "real contents," but this form of reality is still completely homogeneous and undifferentiated. Here the nuances of significance and value which knowledge creates in its concept of the object, which enable it to distinguish different spheres of objects and to draw a line between the world of truth and the world of appearance, are utterly lacking. Myth lives entirely by the presence of its object — by the intensity with which it seizes and takes possession of consciousness in a specific moment . . . . Consciousness is bound by its mere facticity; it possesses neither the impulsion nor the means to correct or criticize what is given here and now, to limit its objectivity by *measuring* it against something not given, something past or future. And if this mediate criterion is absent, all "truth" and reality dissolve into the mere presence of the content, all phenomena are situated on a single plane. Here there are no different *degrees* of reality, no contrasting degrees of objective certainty. The resultant picture of reality lacks the dimension of depth. [pp. 35-6]

This distinction between modes of object-consciousness provides us with a means of distinguishing between various characters in Faulkner's work, and, I believe, with a means of closer analysis of the many characters usually labeled simply "neurotic" — among them, Quentin Compson.

Quentin's reality is homogeneous and undifferentiated. Central to his entire neurosis (I am using the term to indicate an orientation to a reality other than the scientific-empiric reality by which it is judged) is the fixation upon his sister as what amounts to a sacred vessel of chastity or purity. The mythic force of the sacred as opposed to the profane dominates his consciousness of Caddy's sexual character. The contents of his consciousness are ordered by the mythic principle. This principle, says Cassirer,

> is of an entirely different kind and origin from the universal principle of the logical concept. For precisely through their special

character all the contents of the mythical consciousness are rejoined into a whole. They form a self-enclosed realm and possess
a common tonality, by which they are distinguished from the
contents of common, everyday, empirical existence. . . . In their
mere immediate existence they . . . contain a revelation and at the
same time retain a kind of mystery; it is this interpenetration, this
revelation which both reveals and conceals, that gives the mythical-
religious content its basic trait, its character of the "sacred." [p. 74]

While the defiled sanctity of Caddy dominates his mind, images
of another sacred character crop up frequently, the allusions to
the Christian myth.

Quentin's day begins in time. "When the shadow of the sash
appeared on the curtains it was between seven and eight oclock
and then I was in time again, hearing the watch" (p. 93). He
has already determined his suicide and his problem is to live this
last day. His first act is to break the crystal of his watch and
twist the hands off as if to remove himself from the empirical
sequence of time (p. 98). Later he cannot look at the watches
in the jeweler's window until he has satisfied himself by asking
the jeweler that none of them tells the correct time (p. 103).
Although he cannot stop time or turn it back, he can refuse to
acknowledge it and can accept the mockery of confusion the
various wrong timepieces display. It is, in a sense, an act of regres-
sion signaling his total rejection of a world that is now ruled by
the profane element of his private vision, a vision which on this
last day flows through his mind in terms of its destruction through
Caddy's loss of virginity. His rejection of measured time becomes
a part of the mythic construct of his consciousness. ". . . it lies in
the essence of mythical thinking," says Cassirer, "that wherever
it posits a relation, it causes the members of this relation to flow
together and merge. . . . The stages of time — past, present, future
— do not remain distinct; over and over again the mythical consciousness succumbs to the tendency and temptation to level the
differences and ultimately transform them into pure identity."
(Cassirer, pp. 110-11). Time or the attempt to avoid time is
the dominant feature of this particular day of his life and merges
with the other ideas flowing through his mind:

You can be oblivious to the sound [of a watch] for a long while,
then in a second of ticking it can create in the mind unbroken the
long diminishing parade of time you didn't hear. Like Father said
down the long and lonely light-rays you might see Jesus walking,

like. And the good Saint Francis that said Little Sister Death,
that never had a sister. [p. 94]

The allusion to Christ and St. Francis is repeated almost at
once as the chimes strike the hour and then leads into Quentin's
obsession with Caddy's sin:

> Like all the bells that ever rang still ringing in the long dying
> light-rays and Jesus and Saint Francis talking about his sister.
> Because if it were just to hell; if that were all of it. Finished. If
> things just finished themselves. [p. 97]

Faulkner's inclusion of Saint Francis is obviously to gain the easy
relation provided by the mystic's habitual form of address, in this
case especially, "little sister death." Coupled with Jesus here, the
allusions may be meant to suggest an ideal — unattainable or
destroyed, as in Mr. Compson's words recalled by the working
of the watch: "Father said that. That Christ was not crucified:
he was worn away by a minute clicking of little wheels. That had
no sister" (p. 94). The watch again calls forth an allusion, this
time evidently pointing to the absurdities of these ideal images:

> The watch ticked on. I turned the face up, the blank dial with
> little wheels clicking and clicking behind it, not knowing any
> better. Jesus walking on Galilee and Washington not telling lies.
> [pp. 98-9]

Quentin's allusions to the resurrection also reject the promise
offered. His body will not rise, only the flatirons he intends to
use for weights (pp. 98 and 139).

It is the myth of Eden he seems to accept for its suggestions
about the nature of women. And it is his father, Mr. Compson,
who acts as the voice of the scientific empiric mode, attempting
to make Quentin "correct or criticize what is given here and now,
to limit its objectivity by *measuring* it against something not
given, something past or future." As Quentin attempts to recreate
the "homogeneity" of his objective world by fitting in the fact of
Caddy's pregnancy, he attempts to substitute himself for Dalton
Ames in an incest fantasy. "I said I have committed incest,
Father I said" (p. 95).

> In the South you are ashamed of being a virgin. Boys. Men. They
> lie about it. Because it means less to women, Father said. He said

it was men invented virginity not women. Father said it's like death: only a state in which the others are left and I said, But to believe it doesn't matter and he said, That's what's so sad about anything: not only virginity, and I said, Why couldn't it have been me and not her who is unvirgin and he said, That's why that's sad too; nothing is even worth the changing of it. . . . [p. 96]

. . . you are confusing sin and morality women dont do that your Mother is thinking of morality whether it be sin or not has not occurred to her. [p. 126]

But Quentin's mind remains fastened on Caddy and her "sin":

> . . . *the curtains leaning in on the twilight upon the odour of the apple tree her head against the twilight her arms behind her head kimono-winged the voice that breathed o'er eden clothes upon the bed by the nose seen above the apple* [p. 130]

> *The chair-arm flat cool smooth under my forehead shaping the chair the apple tree leaning on my hair above the eden clothes by the nose seen.* [p. 139]

He remembers the confrontations of Caddy, his attempts to preserve the sacred world in which they would be alone together, bridging the two of them into a supernatural world of hell where the fantasy of incest would guarantee their eternal immolation in a substitute purity replacing the purity of nature Benjy found in the smell of trees equated with Caddy and now lost.

The incest motif as it appears in Quentin's monologue is, strangely enough, best explained in another southern novelist's rationale of his own mythmaking as Andrew Lytle discusses the incest motif in his novel *The Velvet Horn*. In a society such as the defeated South, he says, the induced self-consciousness led to a heightened contemplation of self with a consequent withdrawal of the life force. The mythic analogue he cites is that of Adam and Eve experiencing the worlds of cosmos and chaos:

Their expulsion from the earthly paradise seemed to put them into the disorder of chaos. Actually, they were confronted by a natural order which was a multiplicity of the conflicts of opposites. This is not chaos but life as we suffer it, and we fall into it as the child falls into the world. Continuance depended upon the exercise of the will and especially the crafts, not only to survive but to try to restore, to bring together the two halves which make a whole . . . .

It was some years after I had been working on the as yet unnamed

The Velvet Horn that I realized I was treating an aspect of this ancient drama. The brothers and sister, under the guidance of the eldest, withdrew from the stresses of formal society in an effort to return to the prenatural equilibrium of innocence and wholeness. This is an habitual impulse, the refusal to engage in the cooperating opposites that make life. It is also as illusory as any Golden Age, and forbidden by divine and human law. Therefore, it is the grounds for one of the oldest forms of search and conflict. The symbol for this is incest. It need not be fact; but it is symbol . . . . But the actual union between close kin was not my interest. It was the incest of the spirit which seemed my subject, a spiritual condition which inhered within the family itself . . . . And I had my controlling image well fixed in the top part of my head: incest, the act symbolic of wholeness, not the wholeness of innocence but the strain toward a return to this state of being.[16]

In *The Sound and the Fury* we find the same society, the same family conditions. The Compsons, as a family, have lost the life force, perhaps a condition symbolized by the dead end of Benjy and his sterilization and the bachelorhood of Jason. But long before this, Quentin has withdrawn from "the stresses of formal society" and the acceptance of the life force made by Caddy. One of the major themes of his part of the novel is Quentin's desire to return to "the preternatural equilibrium of innocence and wholeness," and his symbol for this is incest, a symbolic incest that will allow him to escape the fallen condition of his world. For Faulkner too there is the understanding that this search is also a search for a removal from time, and Quentin, rejecting the clocks and watches around him, seeks this "understanding." But Faulkner does not accept this symbolic incest as the only possible way to achieve this condition. In the final section, we are presented with Dilsey whose clock rotates its one false hand in a wild mockery of formal time and in Dilsey we find an acceptable compromise with the search for a rejoined, coherent world, a world not of primal innocence, but one in which man can at least endure.

Quentin's nearest encounter with sex has been the interlude with Natalie in the barn when she undertakes to teach him how to "dance sitting down," a lesson which is cut short when Quentin sees Caddy standing in the doorway. His first reaction is to

---

[16]Lytle, "The Working Novelist and the Mythmaking Process," in Henry A. Murray, ed. *Myth and Mythmaking,* New York: Braziller, 1960, pp. 146-47, 151.

translate his psychic reaction to this sex play into an objective equivalent:

> *I jumped hard as I could into the hogwallow the mud yellowed up to my waist stinking I kept on plunging until I fell down and rolled over in it . . . . mud was warmer than the rain it smelled awful.* [pp. 169-70]

Having smeared Caddy with the mud too, they then go to the branch to wash it off, a ritual washing away of sin that Faulkner employs again in the story "There Was a Queen" where Narcissa, having prostituted herself to gain possession of the Snopes letters, returns home and goes down to the branch to let the water flow over her.[17]

The negation of sex finds an objective parallel in the story Versh once told about the man who mutilated himself, but again his father's words attempting to give it all perspective obtrude:

> It's nature is hurting you not Caddy and I said That's just words and he said So is virginity and I said you dont know. [p. 143]
>
> Because women so delicate so mysterious Father said. Delicate equilibrium of periodical filth between two moons balanced. Moons he said full and yellow as harvest moons her hips thighs. [p. 159]

His father's words dissolve into his own as the impurity seizes upon his thoughts: "Liquid putrefaction like drowned things floating like pale rubber flabbily filled getting the odour of honeysuckle all mixed up" (p. 159). The odor of honeysuckle is the point where the two worlds meet — the purity associated with nature and the heavy fecundity which destroys the purity.

In his preparations for suicide, Quentin has come upon some boys watching a large trout from the bridge he intends to jump from. The trout suggests the Ichthus of Christian symbolism by its juxtaposition to Quentin's remark, "And maybe when He says Rise the eyes will come floating up too, out of the deep quiet and the sleep, to look on glory. And after awhile the flat irons would come floating up. I hid them [the irons] under the end of the bridge and went back and leaned on the rail" (p. 144). It is then he first sees the shadow which is the trout and muses:

> *If it could just be a hell beyond that: the clean flame the two of us more than dead. Then you will have only me then only me then the two of us amid the pointing and the horror beyond the clean flame.* [p. 144]

---

[17]*Collected Stories*, New York: Random House, 1950, p. 741.

The fish rises to the surface to lip some Mayflies and the fantasy continues: *"Only you and me then amid the pointing and the horror walled by the clean flame"* (p. 144). Three boys come on to the bridge and explain that the fish cannot be caught; a prize is offered for it, but only "Boston folks" (p. 147) still come out to try. The old trout has become a neighborhood character and has driven all the other fish from the pond. This is where Quentin will die at midnight and if the trout has any symbolic value it would again be the futility and impossibility of Quentin's embracing another myth, a myth that reconciles the discordant elements of his experience by transcending them.

In his aimless wanderings to fill out the day, Quentin picks up in the bread shop the little Italian girl who follows him around. The comic, ironic interlude during which he attempts to rid himself of the girl whom, like Saint Francis, he addresses in the country fashion as "sister" (p. 155) represents the closest Quentin comes on this day to a normal handling of his objective world. But this world misunderstands the relationship as Julio, her brother, chases them down, thinking Quentin is some sexual pervert attempting a relationship with the girl. Quentin's reaction is a rather logical burst of hysteria as he dissolves in laughter (p. 174).

His wanderings on this sunny day have had him constantly relating his progress in terms of his shadow. The shadow in mythical thought is equated with the object casting it. "A man's shadow," says Cassirer, "plays the same role as his image or picture. It is a real part of him and subject to injury; every injury to the shadow affects the man himself. One must not step on a man's shadow for fear of bringing sickness upon him" (Cassirer, p. 42). Leaning over the bridge, Quentin sees his shadow on the water:

> The shadow of the bridge, the tiers of the railing, my shadow leaning flat upon the water, so easily had I tricked it that would not quit me. At least fifty feet it was, and if I only had something to blot it into the water, holding it until it was drowned, the shadow of the package [with the flat irons] like two shoes wrapped up lying on the water. Niggers say a drowned man's shadow was watching for him in the water all the time. [pp. 110-11]

> When I can see my shadow again if not careful that I tricked into the water shall tread again upon my impervious shadow. . . . Trampling my shadow's bones into the concrete with hard heels . . . I walked upon the belly of my shadow. [pp. 118-19]

The image is repeated many times suggesting in mythic terms the self destruction he has already determined upon as his means of meeting a world where

> all men are just accumulations dolls stuffed with sawdust swept up from the trash heaps where all previous dolls had been thrown away the sawdust flowing from what wound in what side that not for me died not. [p. 218]

At a quarter to midnight, he reviews his rationale for suicide which he had discussed with his father, denying the possibility of his world vision existing and rejecting the one posited by his father:

> The three quarters began. The first note sounded, measured and tranquil, serenely peremptory, emptying the unhurried silence for the next one and that's it if people could only change one another forever that way merge like a flame swirling up for an instant then blown cleanly out along the cool eternal dark instead of lying there trying not to think of the swing [where Caddy's lovemaking began] until all cedars came to have that vivid dead smell of perfume that Benjy hated so . . . and he we must just stay awake and see evil done for a little while its not always and i it doesnt have to be even that long for a man of courage . . . and he you wanted to sublimate a piece of natural human folly into a horror and then exorcise it with truth and i it was to isolate her out of the loud world so that it would have to flee us of necessity and then the sound of it would be as though it had never been and he did you try to make her do it [commit incest] and i i was afraid to i was afraid she might and then it wouldnt have done any good but if i could tell you we did it would have been so and then the others wouldnt be so and then the world would roar away and he and now this other [the contemplated suicide] you are not lying now either but you are still blind to what is in yourself to that part of general truth the sequence of natural events and their causes which shadows every mans brow even benjys you are not thinking of finitude you are contemplating an apotheosis in which a temporary state of mind will become symmetrical above the flesh and aware both of itself and of the flesh it will not quite discard. [pp. 219-20]

This attempt to force the scientific-empiric mode of thought upon Quentin has failed and he goes to his death. On June 2, 1910, Quentin rejects not only the empiric-scientific view of the world but the Christian myth that men employ to endure it. Eighteen years later, that myth can only offer the quality of endurance. The celebration of the resurrection does not effect a millennial state; Dilsey may exemplify endurance in terms of the promise held forth by the preacher who has seen the "power en de glory" (p. 371) but hell is not harrowed and the most we find is the world of the lost soul restored to an endurable state, "each in its ordered place."

The original question, What happened to Faulkner when he came to write *The Sound and the Fury?* will probably continue to interest Faulkner critics and occasion other hypotheses. I suggest that his original, if superficial, interest in mythology received some impetus that caused him to incorporate in his style elements that belong to the theory of myth and, in his matter, elements that are taken from the vast body of anthropological speculations on myths and myth formation.

Commenting on Faulkner's distrust of the potentialities of language, Olga Vickery has said that: "One of the basic attitudes running throughout all his work is the view that language and logic act to obscure truth rather than to reveal it."[18] Florence Leaver, in her study of the relation of diction to myth in Faulkner's works, also remarks this distrust:

> Faulkner is extremely conscious of words as tools, although he does not trust them . . . . Perhaps it is this distance between the deed and the word, the idea without form and the form which it must take, however imperfectly, which accounts for Faulkner's intensity, his attempt to make words do more than they can do — to find *logos* for *mythos*.[19]

Faulkner's distrust of the word is as it is used as a tool of scientific-empiric thought restricted by tradition to the creation or communication of a limited world vision, which neither he nor many of his characters share either exclusively or at all. In experimenting with "distorted" visions of objective reality, he has worked forward from Benjy's merely sensuous perception of objective reality to Quentin's mythic configuration with its own coherence, to a configuration such as Jason's which, while reprehensible, would still be considered "sane" in terms of a scientific-empiric

---

[18]*The Novels of William Faulkner,* rev. ed., Baton Rouge: Louisiana State University Press, 1964, p. 8.
[19]"Faulkner: The Word as Principle and Power," *South Atlantic Quarterly,* LVII (Autumn 1958), pp. 464-65.

mode of thought. In his appendix Faulkner calls Jason "The first sane Compson since before Culloden" (p. 420) but at Nagano he spoke of him as "the most vicious character in my opinion I ever thought of."[20] Evidently "sane" has a somewhat pejorative meaning for Faulkner.

In regard to matter, *The Sound and the Fury* represents a further departure from the early novels in that myth allusion is coherently employed as *mythos* in Aristotle's sense of the term. There is also a wider range of mythic reference. While there are fewer allusions to literary myths and the story seems to be dominated by the Christian myth of the resurrection and the older myth of Eden, many details suggest that Faulkner may have been reading some of the anthropological treatises on myth. It is not unlikely, for instance, that in his bookstore experience he would have come across the one volume abridgement of Frazer's *The Golden Bough* which was published in 1922 and reprinted eight times through 1927.[21] Here he might have found the relation between the goddess and the tree inherent in his hamadryad images, tree worship and its association with life forces (pp. 109 ff.), the crime of incest related to the waste land and punishable by death (p. 141), the requirement that a goddess of fertility be supplied with a mate (which might apply to Eula of *The Hamlet*) (p. 141), and citations of the deaths of servants when the king dies (as in the short story "Red Leaves"). The mythic significance of the shadow is given several pages:

> Often he [the savage] regards his shadow or reflection as his soul, or at all events as a vital part of himself, and as such it is necessarily a source of danger to him. For if it is trampled upon, struck, or stabbed, he will feel the injury as if it were done to his person. . . . [p. 189]
>
> We can now understand why it was a maxim both in ancient India and ancient Greece not to look at one's reflection in water, and why the Greeks regarded it as an omen of death if a man dreamed of seeing himself so reflected. They feared that the water-

---

[20]James B. Meriwether and Michael Millgate, eds. *Lion in the Garden: Interviews with William Faulkner, 1926-1962,* New York: Random House, 1968, p. 146.
[21]Sir James Frazer, *The Golden Bough: A Study in Magic and Religion,* New York: Macmillan, 1922. Carvel Collins, speaking before the American Literature Section of the Modern Language Association in New York, December 28, 1967, stated that Faulkner read the one-volume edition of *The Golden Bough* while staying in Sherwood Anderson's apartment in New Orleans early in 1925.

spirits would drag the person's reflection or soul under water, leaving him soulless to perish. [p. 192]

The castration image in *The Sound and the Fury* is much like the description of the self castration of the eunuch priests of Attis (pp. 347-48) and the prostitution of Temple Drake might find some significance in the accounts of religious prostitution of various cults.

> In Armenia the noblest families dedicated their daughters to the service of the goddess Anaitis in her temple of Acilisena, where the damsels acted as prostitutes for a long time before they were given in marriage. Nobody scrupled to take one of these girls to wife when her period of service was over. [p. 331]

There might even be the possibility that the Atthis allusion in *Soldiers' Pay* is to the god Attis who was equated with a tree rather than to the Athis of Ovid's *Metamorphoses*.

The various discussions of resurrection are many, especially in relation to Adonis and the reviving vegetation his resurrection signifies. The killing of the sacred bear is the most obvious parallel that can be found in Faulkner's work; it occurs in Frazer on pages 505-18, 522, 524, and 532-33. The sacred snake that is also found in *Go Down, Moses* is found in Frazer on page 520. And the ceremonies associated with the scapegoat, significant to *Light in August*, are found in pages 542-79.

When questioned about his reading, Faulkner always defended the author's right to make use of anything he had read, but when questioned about specific books he had read, he left no public record of ever having read *The Golden Bough*. This in itself would not rule out the possibility, for his answers to this question were always rather vague, ending in his repeated favor for the Old Testament.

That Faulkner was familiar with the methods of Frazer and his fellows might be inferred from a passage in his essay "Impressions of Japan." He is speaking of the likenesses he has observed in the farming economy:

> And the names are the same names too: Jonathan and Winesap and Delicious; the heavy August foliage is blue-gray with the same spray which we use. But there the resemblance ceases: every single apple enclosed in its twist of paper until that whole tree to this western eye becomes significant and festive and ceremonial like the

symbolical tree of the western rite of Christmas. Only it is more significant here: where in the West there is one small often artificial tree to a family, wrested from the living dirt to be decked in ritual tinsel and then to die as though the tree were not the protagonist of a rite but the victim of a sacrifice, here not one tree to a family but every tree of all is dressed and decked to proclaim and salute older gods than Christ: Demeter and Ceres.[22]

It would seem that in considering the question of Faulkner's sources and their influence upon him in the important period of the late twenties, consideration must be given to his travels in the realms of *The Golden Bough* and similar works.

Faulkner's new-found powers result in what must be regarded as pessimistic expression in *The Sound and the Fury*. Although built around two major mythic images, the novel does not accept the promise inherent in the Christian myth of the fall and the resurrection. On the one hand, he is fully aware of man's potential for making his life a hell; it is the documentation of this activity which constitutes his pessimistic naturalism. It might, in terms of the antithesis I have been using, be equated with a scientific-empiric view of the world. On the other hand, Faulkner has a very optimistic emotional vision of man's estate. After the pronouncements attendant upon the reception of the Nobel prize, there was a critical rush to prove that this positive part of his vision entitled him to the accolade of "traditional moralist," and to fit him into the Christian tradition. Soon after, the publication of *A Fable* wrought consternation among the critics who, examining the theology they found in the novel, found that it was not orthodox Christianity and blamed Faulkner for this "defect." *The Sound and the Fury* illustrates very early that although Faulkner makes much use of the images associated with Christianity he offers no great allegiance to their mythic content. The Christian myths are useful tools, he admits, but they are subordinated in his overall vision to larger mythic ideas, such as the scapegoat and the earth mother images. It is around such vast mythic patterns and not around the narrow, limited myths of any specific culture that his positive ideas of man's estate are organized.

---

[22]James B. Meriwether, ed. *Essays, Speeches & Public Letters by William Faulkner,* New York: Random House, 1966, p. 80.

Carvel Collins

The Interior Monologues of
The Sound and the Fury

William Faulkner built *The Sound and the Fury* on more structural systems than seem yet to have been noticed.[1] In this paper I
shall discuss only two of these systems, chiefly in an attempt to
look more closely at the structure and ordering of the three long
interior monologues, the topic assigned to me.

I believe that Faulkner was indebted in great part to James
Joyce for the idea that a novel could profit from structural systems
which originated outside the novel, as do those which I shall
discuss here. For at least two reasons Faulkner's readers often

From *English Institute Essays 1952,* ed. Alan Downer, (New York: Columbia
University Press, 1954). The original version of this essay was read before
The English Institute in September, 1952, as one of four papers assigned in
a symposium on *The Sound and the Fury.* A somewhat revised version was
included in *Psychoanalysis and American Fiction,* ed. Irving Malin (New
York: Dutton, 1965), and it has been further revised for this collection.
[1]In addition to the additional material incorporated into the present version
of this essay, I have, since 1952, discussed one or more of these systems in
the following places: *New York Times Book Review,* August 1, 8, and 22,
1954; *Princeton University Library Chronicle,* XVIII (Spring 1957); and
The Salzburg Seminar (July 1955) and The English Institute (September
1957).

have not noticed the similarities between some of his methods and the methods of Joyce: Faulkner's use of older literature and of external systems to organize and inform his works has been, as a rule, less readily apparent than Joyce's, perhaps because the pioneering of Joyce had cleared the way and demonstrated the method and T. S. Eliot's famous review of *Ulysses* had done much to publicize it so that a follower could use it less obviously. Secondly, Faulkner, in a characteristically ironic, self-protective way, has convinced a number of literary men not only that he is ill-read but also that he never really plans a work of fiction.

In *The Sound and the Fury* Faulkner's literary debt to *Ulysses* and to *A Portrait of the Artist as a Young Man* is extremely clear. His adaptation of Joyce's interior monologue is, of course, a major indebtedness. And smaller but significant debts at once come to mind, among them the similarities between the alleged attitudes of the elder Dedalus and of Mr. Compson toward the families of their wives or between the inaccurate Compson kitchen clock which Dilsey can interpret and the inaccurate Dedalus clock which the women of the family can interpret though Stephen cannot or the numerous similarities between Quentin Compson and the Stephen Dedalus of both the *Portrait* and *Ulysses*. Even more basic to *The Sound and the Fury* are its structural systems, the concepts of which I believe came from Joyce.[2] Of these several systems I want to discuss two.

By the title of *Ulysses* Joyce had guided his readers' attention to Homer's *Odyssey*, and he had used the *Odyssey* as a structural frame against which to place the events of a day in early twentieth-century Dublin. In one section the reader finds himself, for example, not only in a Dublin newspaper office but also in Homer's cave of the winds. Though readers can get much enjoyment from *Ulysses* without detailed knowledge of this structural scheme, sensitive and sophisticated readers of Joyce get increased aesthetic enjoyment because critics have pointed it out to them. I believe that Faulkner drew similar parallels and that though readers can also enjoy *The Sound and the Fury* without a "key" it is aesthetically profitable to point out the presence of its various, masterfully interlocked structural systems.

---

[2]In his interesting interview with Jean Stein in 1956, Faulkner stated "You should approach Joyce's *Ulysses* as the illiterate Baptist preacher approaches the Old Testament: with faith." James B. Meriwether and Michael Millgate, eds. *Lion in the Garden: Interviews with William Faulkner, 1926-1962* (New York: Random House, 1968), p. 250.

Like Joyce, Faulkner presents the title of his novel as an indication that he has taken some of its form from an older work of literature, here, of course, the famous speech in the fifth scene of the fifth act of *Macbeth*:

> Out, out, brief candle!
> Life's but a walking shadow, a poor player
> That struts and frets his hour upon the stage
> And then is heard no more: it is a tale
> Told by an idiot, full of sound and fury,
> Signifying nothing.

It seems possible to demonstrate that several elements of *The Sound and the Fury* stem from a systematic exploitation of this Shakespearean passage. The first and major account of the Compson family's failure is in the opening monologue of the idiot Benjamin. Readers who look chiefly for plot in a novel have suggested that *The Sound and the Fury* would be more effective if the first monologue were not the idiot's, but Jason's. Aside from a number of other objections to making this change, the chief of which will be offered in another connection later in this paper, I think that Macbeth's speech, in its emphasis on life as "a tale told by an idiot," was alone almost sufficient reason, in Faulkner's mind, to present Benjamin's monologue first. The Shakespeare passage seems not only to have suggested to Faulkner the possibility of having an idiot tell the essential tale which would begin the novel but also may have contributed to his representation of the idiot as the main figure at the novel's conclusion.

I believe that Faulkner also drew on the Shakespeare passage for elements of the content of the three interior monologues. "Out, out, brief candle!" is a central device in the treatment of Benjamin. As many scenes in the first monologue show, the idiot's chief source of pleasure and comfort after the departure of his sister Candace is firelight, which he sees as "smooth, bright shapes" fascinating and comforting him. One of several illustrations demonstrating that his associates have come to know that firelight will soothe him occurs when he is crying after having hurt his hand. Dilsey immediately says, " 'Here, look at the fire. Dilsey make your hand stop hurting in just a minute. Look at the fire.' She opened the fire door." And firelight as a pleasure and comfort for Benjamin is specifically associated with candlelight in a passage involving candles which are both "brief" in physical length and "brief" in their pleasant shining for Benjamin before they are extinguished. Dilsey has bought with her own money a cheap cake for Benjamin's thirty-third birthday. "She lit the candles on the cake. Some of them were little ones. Some were big ones cut into little pieces." Dilsey, who fears that Jason, Benjamin's cruelly oppressive and joyless brother, will interfere with even this inexpensive pleasure, hastens the shoddy festival, telling Benjamin and his attendant, Luster, " 'You all go ahead and eat this cake, now, before Jason come.' " When she steps out of the kitchen, Luster immediately "leaned down and puffed his face. The candles went away. I began to cry. 'Hush,' Luster said. 'Here. Look at the fire whiles I cuts this cake.' "

The second interior monologue, Quentin's, owes one of its often repeated motifs to the statement by Macbeth which immediately follows the imperative about the candle: "Life's but a walking shadow." After the concluding sentence of Benjamin's monologue, with its final reference to smooth, bright shapes, Quentin's monologue begins, its first sentence containing the word "shadow." This word recurs at least forty-five times in Quentin's monologue, more than a third of these instances being associated with movement, often walking: "I walked upon my shadow"; "I walked upon the belly of my shadow"; "our shadows running along the wall"; "I stepped on my shadow"; "Trampling my shadow's bones into the concrete with hard heels"; "treading my shadow into pavement"; "trampling my shadow into the dust"; "my shadow pacing me"; "watching the shadow move. It moved almost perceptibly, creeping back inside the door."

The actions of Jason, the third and final monologist, presumably continue the pattern of Macbeth's speech. Jason is certainly "a poor player That struts and frets his hour upon the stage." All three brothers move restlessly, but Jason's restlessness is the most pronounced and the most fretful as he dashes about the town and the countryside. And despite the decline of his family's fortunes and his own he struts upon the stage before his associates, telling them, for example, that "my people owned slaves here when you all were running little shirt tail country stores and farming land no nigger would look at on shares."

Considerably more important than this sustained parallel to Shakespeare's passage is another system of Joycean parallelism in *The Sound and the Fury*. Joyce had based *Ulysses* not only on a literary work but also on human anatomy, the sections of his novel being associated with now the brain, now the esophagus, now the heart, and so forth; the Dublin newspaper office, to return to the example used above, is not only associated with the cave of the winds but also with the lungs. Faulkner seems to me similarly, whether or not imitating this *particular* parallelism by Joyce, to have organized the three interior monologues not on the chart of human anatomy but on a chart of human personality — and the chart was the one drawn up by Freud.

I submit that in writing *The Sound and the Fury* Faulkner carefully, consciously, and creatively drew much of the form and content of the three long interior monologues from Freudian theory: The monologue of Benjamin the idiot he drew from Freud's concept of the Id, that of Quentin the suicide from Freud's concept of the Ego, and that of censorious Jason from Freud's concept of the Super-ego. As the decades have passed, it has been considered in some quarters less and less sophisticated to speak of Id, Ego, and Super-ego, or even of Freud; but we must remember here that Faulkner published *The Sound and the Fury* in 1929.

On the chance that readers may say Faulkner could not have known about Freud when he was writing *The Sound and the Fury*, I should point out that he not only could have known about Freud but did. Entirely apart from any reading of the Freudian texts, he was exposed to a great deal of talk about Freud's theories during the period he spent in the mid-1920's as one of the New Orleans literary group of which Sherwood Anderson was then the most famous. Though biographers of Anderson fail to agree on whether or not Anderson had read much Freudian theory, he did speak about it; and members of the New Orleans group with which Anderson and Faulkner associated have told me that they naturally were much interested by Freudian theory in those days of its first major impact on American literature and that their talk was full of it, as one might expect. Even if we were to accept the common, absurd assumption that William Faulkner does not read widely, we could find in his New Orleans months sufficient opportunity for him to have heard and absorbed the elements of Freud's pattern. But it is safe also to assume not only that he listened to Freudian theory but that from his wide and continuous reading he learned about it as well. In addition, Phil Stone, Faulkner's close associate of that period, has told me that he and Faulkner talked at length about the theories of Freud.

One other probable objection must be dealt with briefly here. Many critics and readers have a prejudice against the use of psychological theory in literary criticism. They are not without justification, for too often psychological literary criticism has been the result of efforts by amateurs in psychology to probe the personalities of authors. Studies of that sort by trained psychoanalysts should be encouraged. But I want to stress here that the

following remarks are in no sense psychoanalytical, that they are
not an attempt to probe William Faulkner's psyche, and that
although a source from which he consciously drew important
elements of the form and content of *The Sound and the Fury*
seems to me to be Freudian theory I am here examining his
deliberate use of that source as I would if the source were a
phrenology manual, "Gunga Din," or *The Iliad*.

In the following discussion all quotations of Freudian theory
and references to it are from books in print in English before
Faulkner completed *The Sound and the Fury*. Among the books
readily available to him, naturally, was *The Encyclopædia Britannica*, in the 1926 edition of which the famous article on "Psycho-
analysis," written by Sigmund Freud himself, described Freud's
concept of the elements of personality as follows:

> *Topographically,* psychoanalysis regards the mental apparatus as
> a composite instrument, and endeavours to determine at what points
> in it the various mental processes take place. According to most
> recent psychoanalytic views, the mental apparatus is composed of
> an *"id,"* which is the reservoir of the instinctive impulses, of an
> *"ego,"* which is the most superficial portion of the id and one which
> is modified by the influence of the external world, and of a *"super-
> ego,"* which develops out of the id, dominates the ego and represents
> the inhibitions of instinct characteristic of man.

In a book translated and easily available at the time Faulkner
was preparing *The Sound and the Fury*, Freud also said:

> From the point of view of morality, the control and restriction of
> instinct, it may be said of the id that it is totally non-moral, of the
> ego that it strives to be moral, and of the super-ego that it can be
> hyper-moral and then becomes ruthless.

In statements such as these we can see taking form large elements of the general pattern of the three interior monologues,
which I should like now to examine individually in some detail
after one additional disclaimer. Faulkner was writing a novel, not
drawing a diagram. He may have assigned their roles to the three
monologists, Benjamin and Quentin and Jason, in accordance
with Freudian topography — as well as with other external systems not under discussion here — but he did not allow these
characters to be stiff and inhuman as a result. They are three-
dimensional beings containing a surprising amount of "felt life,"
and in his ability to make them come alive despite — or perhaps

because of — their symbolic chores Faulkner shows his genius. It is important for readers to remember that Faulkner was not writing *The Sound and the Fury* to illustrate Freud's theory and so had no obligation to present every one of its subtleties.

An idiot much like Benjamin Compson appeared in Faulkner's fiction before the publication of *The Sound and the Fury*, in his 1925 New Orleans *Times-Picayune* sketch titled "The Kingdom of God." That idiot, like Benjamin Compson, had eyes

clear and blue as cornflowers, and utterly vacant of thought . . . a shapeless, dirty lump, life without mind, an organism without intellect. Yet always in his slobbering, vacuous face were his two eyes of a heart-shaking blue, and gripped tightly in one fist was a narcissus.

After brief mistreatment by a man not entirely unlike Jason Compson and defense by a brother not unlike Quentin, the idiot in the story ends his Benjamin-like bellows when his broken narcissus, like Benjamin's, is repaired by splints, and like Benjamin in the final scene of *The Sound and the Fury*, he disappears "down the street, and so from sight, the ineffable blue eyes of the idiot dreaming above his narcissus clenched tightly in his dirty hand."

Faulkner's greatly expanded treatment of this figure in the first interior monologue of *The Sound and the Fury* shows a remarkable number of parallels with the Freudian concept of the Id. The fact that Freud considered the Id to be that part of the human personality which is first to be formed ("To the oldest of the mental provinces or agencies we give the name of *id*") may be one reason Faulkner placed Benjamin's interior monologue at the beginning of the novel rather than in its chronological position as the third of the novel's four sections. Ernest Jones, a leading disciple of Freud, had published three editions of a volume of *Papers on Psycho-Analysis*, which *The Encyclopædia Britannica*, at the end of Freud's article quoted above, recommended to English-speaking readers as "Particularly accessible." In those *Papers* Jones listed and discussed the characteristics which Freud attributed to the unconscious. There is support for my assumption that Faulkner, for his novelistic purposes, did not need to bother about the technicalities differentiating unconscious and Id, for Freud himself had written that he proposed to begin by "giving to the other part of the mind, into which [the Ego] extends and which behaves as though it were Ucs [that is, the unconscious] the name of *Id*." Jones's account of Freud's theories said that the unconscious is close to the primary instincts and that without the refining efforts of education each of us "would probably remain a selfish, jealous, impulsive, aggressive, dirty, immodest, cruel, egocentric, and conceited animal, inconsiderate of the needs of others, and unmindful of the complicated social and ethical standards." Though some readers, because of their sympathy for the badly misused Benjamin thoughtlessly regard him as an admirable moralist of some sort, Faulkner actually gives him these unattractive characteristics. He is "selfish": he thinks only of his own desires, and we never see him performing any act for others. He is "jealous": when Candace puts on perfume for the first time, first kisses one of the town boys, and later loses her virginity, Benjamin's bellows arise not from moral judgment but from his selfish and jealous awareness that he is losing a gratification because Candace is growing away from him. He is certainly "impulsive" and he is "aggressive," bellowing his discontent and at times acting as aggressively as his associates and circumstances permit, the outstanding example being his encounter with the schoolgirl in his desire to regain Candace. He is "dirty": "*Has he got to keep that old dirty slipper on the table . . . Why dont you feed him in the kitchen. It's like eating with a pig.*" He is "immodest," not hesitating to display his unfortunate sexual mutilation. He is "egocentric" and "inconsiderate of the needs of others and unmindful of . . . social and ethical standards." He is not shown to be particularly "cruel" unless we so interpret his frightening behavior toward the schoolgirl, nor is he "conceited" unless we so interpret his behavior during the scenes in which he wants Candace to remain with him, the drooling idiot, rather than go on to develop into normal adulthood and find another man to love.

Jones's volume also states one of Freud's concepts of the Id which Faulkner put to important technical use in the monologue of the Compson idiot: that the unconscious mental processes "have no relation whatever to the idea of time." A main characteristic of Benjamin's monologue is its demonstration that he has no sense of time: his mind jumps freely from one memory to another no matter how much time separates them, ranging rapidly back and forth among scenes scattered over many years.

Jones gives other features of the unconscious which are also Benjamin's. Both are "isolated from outer reality." Both are "exceedingly mobile," Benjamin not only shifting quickly from scene to scene of his memories but also just as quickly and easily shifting from happy to sad to happy again. An example of Benjamin's mobility of emotion is an episode in the courthouse square. When the carriage was following its usual route, he "sat, holding the flower in his fist, his gaze empty and untroubled." When Luster turned the carriage contrary to ritual, Benjamin for "an instant" sat "in an utter hiatus. Then he bellowed. Bellow on bellow . . . it was horror; shock." Then the carriage started moving conventionally again "and at once" Benjamin "hushed" and became "serene."

Jones wrote: "The infantile character of the unconscious . . . persists throughout the whole of life." Benjamin reverts to childhood in most of his memories; and in every physical aspect except his size he has remained there, being tended and fed as though he were an infant: " 'How old he.' 'He thirty-three.' Luster said . . . 'You mean, he been three years old thirty years.' " Though Benjamin's monologue moves back and forth through many memories, he concludes it with a memory of going to sleep in the evening of the earliest day which he recalls from his childhood.

Benjamin, like the idiot in "The Kingdom of God," carries a narcissus. This may be just chance, of course, but in a novel otherwise so elaborately planned it seems reasonable to assume that the author intended Benjamin's flower to have some significance.[3] Faulkner certainly shows us that the elemental Benjamin is narcissistic, and Freud had written that "narcissism is the universal original condition" and had dealt at length with what he called "the primary infantile narcissism."

The unconscious, according to Jones's *Papers*, has "a logic of its own, but this is . . . of the emotions and not of the reason." In an early book Freud had said, "The id . . . has its own world of perception." Benjamin is shown to have special logic and perception, which seem uncanny to his associates. "He smell what you tell him when he want to. Don't have to listen nor talk." And elsewhere: " 'He know lot more than folks thinks,' Roskus said. 'He knowed they time was coming, like that pointer done.' " And Benjamin can tell when Candace has been kissed for the first time and when she has just lost virginity and is moving

---

[3]Faulkner's reply to a question on this subject is a good illustration of his responses to questioning about his works. When he was asked in a 1956 *Paris Review* interview, "Does the narcissus given to Benjy have some significance?" Faulkner replied, "The narcissus was given to Benjy to distract his attention. It was simply a flower which happened to be handy . . . It was not deliberate." (*Lion in the Garden*, p. 246.)

farther and farther away from her close association with him: "Her eyes flew at me, and away. I began to cry. It went loud and I got up . . . I went toward her, crying, and she shrank against the wall and I saw her eyes and I cried louder."

Freud said that the Id "cannot say what it wants." Benjamin is inarticulate and always unsuccessful when he is "trying to say." That he is inarticulate is stated explicitly in the novel: " 'He cant talk.' Charlie said."

Freud had written, "Thinking in pictures is . . . a very incomplete form of becoming conscious. . . . it approximates more closely to unconscious processes than does thinking in words, and it is unquestionably older than the latter." A sample of Benjamin's thinking in pictures is his observation of Miss Quentin's final departure from the Compson house:

> *It came out of Quentin's window and climbed across into the tree.*
> *We watched the tree shaking. The shaking went down the tree,*
> *then it came out and we watched it go away across the grass.*

Benjamin operates as a camera and recording machine; we know that he is far removed from articulating his interior monologue when Faulkner shows him to be capable of reproducing his father's remark, " '*Et ego in arcadia.*' "

Jones reported that the unconscious "consists of repressed mental material," and in Freudian theory the Id is constantly subject to confinement and restriction. In *The Sound and the Fury* Benjamin is constantly watched, controlled, and confined. The first words of his monologue, which are the first words of the novel, tell us that he is looking "through the fence." He later remembers when Candace was married and went away forever: "Then they were running and I came to the corner of the fence . . . I held to the fence, looking after them and trying to say" (p. 63). His attendants are repeatedly told to keep him restricted: " 'Keep him in the yard, now' "; " '*Didn't they told you not to take him off the place.*' " This motif of the fence I should like to return to in the discussion of Jason's monologue.

That part of the personality immediately beyond the Id in Freud's pattern is the Ego; beyond the Ego and last to develop is the Super-ego. Faulkner arranged the monologues of *The Sound and the Fury* so that they follow this scheme — at the expense of their chronological order as indicated by the date at the head of each monologue. Because the Ego is between two of its "masters," Id and Super-ego, and in Faulkner's use of it clearly serves as a battleground for them, I shall momentarily postpone discussion of Quentin's Ego-like monologue to discuss Jason's monologue and its apparent debt to Freud's conception of the Super-ego.

As Freud conceived the Super-ego it "represents the inhibitions of instinct," as he had put it in his article in the 1926 *Britannica*, going on to say further that there "is a force in the mind which exercises the functions of a censorship, and which excludes from consciousness and from any influence upon action all tendencies which displease it." Freud elsewhere had said, "The super-ego may bring fresh needs to the fore, but its chief function remains the *limitation* of satisfactions." In addition, Freud and his commentators had characterized the Super-ego as energetic, severe even to cruelty, independent, and in some ways aloof, yet concerned about public opinion and gradually taking over the role of the parents, being that part of the personality more closely associated with them.

Jason Compson IV has these characteristics. He is named for his father and is associated with him in trying to keep the idiot restrained. Of all the children he is the closest to the mother. At one point she says, "I must go away you keep the others I'll take Jason . . . the only one my heart went out to without dread." Later she tells Jason, "You are the only one of them that isn't a reproach to me," and she continues to make such remarks throughout the novel. Jason is even shown to be not only associated more closely than the other children with his mother but with his grandmother as well.

Jason takes over with a vengeance his parents' controlling functions. He urges his father to send Benjamin to the state asylum; when the father refuses, Jason plans to send Benjamin there as soon as he himself is fully in charge of the family. After the father's death we see Jason take up his role as head of the family and steadily usurp his mother's authority over the household, especially over Benjamin and their wayward niece. "If you want me to control her, just say so and keep your hands off," he tells his mother. In a violent scene he at last takes over completely, snatching his mother's keys in order to examine his niece's room, though his mother wails to the servant that "I never let anyone take my keys."

From the start Jason is independent and aloof, after the fashion of the Super-ego as Freudian theory had described it. In the earliest episode recorded in the novel we see the Compson children playing in a stream. "Jason was playing too. He was by himself further down the branch." Other early scenes present him as an informer when the others have transgressed parental orders, as in the childhood episode when Candace and Quentin play and struggle in the stream. He also refuses to accept any authority delegated to Candace: " '[Father] said to mind me.' Caddy said. 'I'm not going to mind you.' Jason said." When they become older, Jason ruthlessly blocks each of Candace's wishes.

Throughout the scenes of family life we see Jason set apart, yet as the years pass he shows himself to be interested in public opinion, violently repressing those members of his family who attract unfavorable attention from the town. He wants Benjamin kept out of the town's sight pending Mrs. Compson's death and the opportunity to send him out of sight permanently. He asks Benjamin's attendant, "What the hell makes you want to keep him around here where people can see him?" He is furious with his niece for the lack of secrecy in her promiscuity:

> Like I say it's not that I object to so much; maybe she cant help that, it's because she hasn't even got enough consideration for her own family to have any discretion. I'm afraid all the time I'll run into them right in the middle of the street . . . like a couple of dogs."

Earlier he is angry, with

> the position I try to uphold to have her with no more respect for what I try to do for her than to make her name and my name and my Mother's name a byword in the town . . .[4]

---

[4]The author of a well-known handbook on Faulkner makes the following statement about the thesis which this paper introduced into Faulkner criticism:
"Freudian critics view the first three sections of the novel as representations of the id, the ego, and the super-ego. The idea is interesting and appealing, but describing Jason as a representative of the super-ego seems to me a distortion for the sake of a thesis. As I show in my analysis, Jason is alienated from his entire society and he is governed by irrational forces." (Edmond L. Volpe, *A Reader's Guide to William Faulkner* [New York: Noonday Press, 1964], p. 406.)
The reply to this would seem to be: (*a*) for a critic to propose that Faulkner *consciously* used one of Freud's constructions while writing the three monologues of *The Sound and the Fury* does not make the critic "Freudian"; (*b*) the passages just quoted from the novel, as well as several others not quoted, demonstrate that Jason, though distorted and unpleasant and unsocial, is not "alienated from his entire society" but is, in a very ill way, quite concerned with his society's opinion; and (*c*) the psychoanalytical works available to Faulkner made clear that Freud conceived of the super-ego as often "governed by irrational forces."

Jason is extremely severe and cruel in his repression of freedom and pleasure. Even his mother thinks he is too brutal. He is physically and mentally cruel to his niece. He favors poisoning the pigeons in the square even if the poison will also kill dogs. His method with women is to "keep them guessing. If you cant think of any other way to surprise them, give them a bust in the jaw." He is angry that a tent show has brought enjoyment to the town. He sadistically burns two show tickets before the longing eyes of Benjamin's young attendant, who has no ticket money. Throughout Jason's monologue we see him spending enormous amounts of energy in this concentration upon repressive thoughts and acts and — to use the phrase Freud had used to describe the chief function of the Super-ego — upon "the *limitation* of satisfactions."

Like his two brothers, Jason seems obsessed by their loving sister Candace. But in keeping with Freud's theories, whereas Benjamin longs for her and Quentin is simultaneously attracted and repelled, Jason undeviatingly dislikes her. Candace's promiscuity, which resulted in the illegitimate birth of her daughter and caused her husband to divorce her, costs Jason his chance for a socially respected position in Candace's husband's bank; so Jason finally takes out his hatred of the absent Candace on her daughter, seeing in her "the very symbol of the lost job itself."

It seems to me that one of the novel's important episodes, involving Jason and Benjamin and referred to many times in the book from different points of view, owes its essence and probably even its presence in the novel to Faulkner's conscious and deliberate construction of Benjamin and Jason in part on the lines of Freud's concepts of Id and Super-ego. Much is made in the novel, from its opening page to its final paragraph, of Jason's attempt to keep Benjamin confined within the fence which surrounds the Compson yard. When thus confined Benjamin is shown to spend part of his time at the gate hoping to get out to seek the gratification he associates with his departed sister. One day the gate is left unlatched. Benjamin goes through it, molests a schoolgirl, and is knocked down by the girl's father. Benjamin then receives a punishment out of the Freudian textbook: Freud had written that "castration is probably the kernel around which the subsequent fear of conscience has gathered," conscience having been equated to the Super-ego earlier in the passage. This episode at the gate in the fence within which Jason wants to keep Benjamin confined conceivably stems from Freud's idea that the

Super-ego or conscience stands as censor at the portal between unconscious and conscious to prevent the Id or the unconscious from passing through to achieve its desires. As Freud presented his model of this situation: "The crudest conception of these systems is the one we shall find most convenient, a spatial one. The unconscious system may therefore be compared to a larger anteroom." Adjoining this anteroom or enclosure is the room or enclosure of consciousness, but

> between the two there stands a personage with the office of door-keeper, who examines the various mental excitations, censors them, and denies them admittance to the reception-room when he disapproves of them . . . Now I know very well that you will say that these conceptions are as crude as they are fantastic . . . Still, I should like to assure you that these crude hypotheses, the two chambers, the door-keeper on the threshold between the two . . . must indicate an extensive approximation to the actual reality.

Having glanced at the first and third monologists, let us go back now to Quentin, the second monologist and the one who, I believe, received part of his characterization from Freud's conception of the Ego. An idea of Freud's would seem a likely source for one of the most significant technical differences between the first two monologues: After Freud, as noted above, had said that the Id possesses no sense of time, he went on to say that it is the Ego which "arranges the processes of the mind in a temporal order." Benjamin's monologue, as we have seen, shows him to have no awareness whatever of time. But Quentin's monologue shows that Quentin is not only aware of but obsessed by time, both real and symbolic. Faulkner further dramatizes this difference between these two brothers at the point in the novel where the first monologue, the idiot Benjamin's, ends and the second monologue, Quentin's, begins: Benjamin's fluid, timeless jumping back and forth in his memories ends with a memory of his going to sleep one night; in the next sentence of the novel Quentin begins his monologue by saying night has ended and he is now "in time again."

Freud had presented other characteristics of the Ego as follows: "The instincts in the id press for immediate satisfaction, regardless of all else, and in this way either fail of achievement or actually do damage. It is the ego's task to avert these mishaps, to mediate between the pretensions of the id and the pretensions of the outer world." Yet as "the child was once compelled to obey its parents, so the ego submits to the categorical imperative pronounced by its super-ego." Therefore "we see this same ego as a poor creature owing service to three masters and consequently menaced by three several dangers: from the external world, from the libido of the id, and from the severity of the super-ego." The personality of Quentin, the most rounded and least schematic of the three brothers, seems to be in large part based on these psychological concepts: like Benjamin he wants his sister, like Jason he rejects that desire, and like a weak Ego he is unable to cope with this conflict.

After the original publication of this paper it occurred to me that Faulkner had presented this situation in more diagrammatic form during 1926 when he wrote his unpublished forty-eight-page novelette titled *Mayday*. This seems even more a forerunner of Quentin's monologue than "The Kingdom of God" seems a forerunner of Benjamin's, and it might be well to discuss it briefly here as supportive evidence that Faulkner was capable of writing *The Sound and the Fury* in the way this paper suggests he did.

The Sound and the Fury is a post-Joycean allegory, in which the surface story is fully realistic; *Mayday* is an allegory of an older type in which the surface is unreal and many of the characters bear names bluntly signifying their functions. In *Mayday* while Sir Galwyn, the young knight who is the forerunner of Quentin Compson, moves through a landscape much like that of Poictesme, he is accompanied by a green figure on horseback named Hunger and a red figure on horseback named Pain. They hold the same positions in relation to Sir Galwyn that their later counterparts, the yearning Benjamin and the castigating Jason, hold to Quentin while the three monologists face the reader from the platform of *The Sound and the Fury*: Hunger, like Benjamin, is on Sir Galwyn's right hand, and Pain, like Jason, is on his left. Quentin Compson is drawn to his sister by a hunger like that of Benjamin, and he is painfully drawn away from her by restrictions like those of Jason; similarly Sir Galwyn is pulled and hauled by his two allegorical companions as he experiences love, converses with a character named Time whose disillusioned remarks are like those which Mr. Compson makes to Quentin, and meets St. Francis of Assisi, of whom Quentin was to speak in his interior monologue. Finally Sir Galwyn, like Quentin, escapes the tension of Hunger and Pain by drowning himself in a river. Even those critics who persist in regarding Faulkner as a rather conventional realist who merely had a difficult style will have to agree that, if nothing else, *Mayday* demonstrates that he was capable at least once of using allegory when writing about a character in Quentin Compson's general situation.

During recent years I have found that in writing *The Sound and the Fury* Faulkner often drew on his own childhood. He had called his maternal grandmother "Damuddy." He knew a Negro servant who had many of the characteristics of the fictional Dilsey. One of his brothers had a pony named Fancy like the fictional Compsons' pony. The physical setting of the area about South Street in Oxford, Mississippi, during the early years of this century and the associations as children between Faulkner and his relatives and neighbors there — though by no means identical with the setting or, certainly, with the relationships and characterizations of Quentin, Benjamin, Jason and Caddy — gave him material for many elements of the fictional lives and characters of the Compson children. These facts, which are to be more fully presented elsewhere, in no way reduce the possibility that when writing *The Sound and the Fury* Faulkner consciously made elaborate use of techniques learned from Joyce and of structures taken from Freud and others.

Freud wrote that the Ego "throws a disguise over the id's conflicts with reality and, if possible, over its conflicts with the super-ego too." Quentin disguises his concern over his desire for his sister Candace by elevating it to a pessimistic philosophy. He seems to use watches and clocks as symbols of philosophical or ethical systems which have guided others but are not able to speak to him with any meaning. He says that they are "Contradicting one another." When he removes the hands from his grandfather's watch as he begins to carry out his plan to kill himself, I take his action to symbolize not only his abandonment of life, in which time is an essential, but also his abandonment of all search for philosophical consolation; he is now fully committed to death from the start of his monologue. Freud had written often of watches and clocks as symbols of femininity; it is probable that even in presenting this aspect of Quentin's sublimation of his desire for Candace, Faulkner is consciously using "Freudian symbols," and using them with great skill. Certainly elsewhere in the book Faulkner seems to use such publicized symbols as pistol, door, slipper, bank, and tree with awareness of the significance which Freud had reported that they often held for patients he had psychoanalyzed.

Incest and such related matters as the Oedipus complex took up much space in the accounts of Freudian theory available to

Faulkner. One remark by Freud may suffice here: "A boy may take his sister as love-object in place of his faithless mother . . . A little girl takes an older brother as a substitute for the father." In our tendency to avoid the subject of incest we must not be led, even by the confusing "Appendix" which Faulkner wrote many years after the novel, into thinking that the feeling between Quentin and his sister Candace is entirely on some high moral or philosophical plane above the incestuous, much as Quentin tries to put it there. Quentin's recurrent memories of his experiences with Candace and of his jealousies document for us how he feels for her. And Candace certainly returns this feeling, as her fiancé testifies when he tells Quentin that Candace

> talked about you all the time . . . I got pretty jealous. . . . I dont mind telling you it never occurred to me it was her brother she kept talking about she couldnt have talked about you any more if you'd been the only man in the world husband wouldnt have been in it.

Quentin has tried to reconcile his difficult conflict between desire and control as a healthy Ego might hope to do, but Freud had pointed out that the Super-ego "often enough succeeds in driving the ego into death, if the latter does not protect itself from the tyrant in time." The conflict between his Benjamin-like hunger for Candace and his Jason-like repression of this forbidden feeling proving too much for him, Quentin by the time he begins his monologue has taken over in an extreme fashion the punishing function of the Super-ego and sets out to kill himself. Freud said that often the Ego is weak and finds it difficult to act. Quentin is shown to be weak in action. He faints in conflict with the potent Dalton Ames. Only when the pressures mount to great intensity following Candace's wedding is Quentin able to bring himself to the act of suicide.

To glance briefly here at a technical matter, the styles of the three monologues seem to me to support the assertion I am making that the three monologists are based in part on Freud's conception of the Id, the Ego, and the Super-ego. Benjamin, as pointed out above, after the fashion of the Id as Freud defined it, cannot speak; and the style of his monologue clearly shows this by its unconventionality. Jason, in a way which fits his partial origin in Freud's conception of the Super-ego as the latest formed of the parts of the human personality and the one closest to the parents and to the social tradition, presents almost all of his monologue in conventional, colloquial syntax and seems to be speaking it aloud, fully articulated like the soliloquy of an actor in a play. Quentin, pulled like the Ego back and forth by conflicting forces, is the only one of the monologists who continually alternates between two distinct styles: when he is compulsively but systematically going about the business of preparing to destroy himself, he soliloquizes, Jason-like, in conventional syntax and could be conventionally understood if he were speaking aloud; when into his thoughts surge memories of Candace and of the odor of honeysuckle which he equates with sexual desire, his monologue takes on a new, second, style which is unconventionally jagged and is very similar to Benjamin's.

The Sound and the Fury has seemed to many literary essayists to be a sociological and economic study of the decay of a family of Southern aristocrats confronted by rising commercialism. As such it is certainly a dull and, to measure it by such Naturalistic conceptions, uninformative novel; surely its attraction for its numerous admirers must be based on more than that. It seems to me to present a larger unit of thought and feeling, more significant, and more generally applicable: I think the novel is concerned not with the sociological but with the psychological and that it moves us by the tragedy which accompanies the Compson family's confusion about love.

The three monologues clearly demonstrate to the reader the effect which the failure of the Compson family has on the sons, whether we regard the three monologists on a realistic level as individuals or on a symbolic level as parts of the personality of one symbolic offspring of the Compsons. All three of the sons (or, if you will permit, all three parts of the one symbolic composite[5]) are injured by lack of love. Quentin says that what Mrs. Compson has interpreted as her husband's contempt for her family has hurt her and that whether or not the contempt existed or was

---

[5]An elaborate and sustained parallel in *The Sound and the Fury* — with Christ's Passion — makes the role of each monologist tightly, though inversely, parallel with the role which Christ played on the day indicated by the date at the head of that particular monologue; so in this structural system also the three monologists are, in a sense, part of one personality. It might be well here to point out that though Candace does not have a monologue and so is not properly part of the assigned subject of this paper, her characterization and her actions bear a striking novelistic similarity to Freud's description of the developing Libido, which, in view of Freud's concept of its role, would logically lead Faulkner not to give Candace a monologue in the novel but to make her the center of attention for all three monologists and thus contribute her share in making of the four Compson children one symbolic personality, unfortunately deprived and twisted.

justified, the damage was *"Done in Mother's mind though. Finished. Finished. Then we were all poisoned."* This novel of poisoning shows Mrs. Compson to be insufficiently loving to her children. Quentin's monologue speaks often of the children's lack of a mother. Very near the end of his monologue Quentin is quite explicit about the failure of both parents:

> When I was little there was a picture in one of our books, a dark place into which a single weak ray of light came slanting upon two faces lifted out of the shadow. *You know what I'd do if I were King?* [Candace] never was a queen or a fairy she was always a king or a giant or a general *I'd break that place open and drag them out and I'd whip them good* It was torn out, jagged out. I was glad. I'd have to turn back to it until the dungeon was Mother herself she and Father upward into weak light holding hands and us lost somewhere below even them without even a ray of light.

As a result of the lack of support from their cold, hypochondriac mother and their warmer but cynical and alcoholic father, all three monologists are hurt in ways which fit the psychological roles which I think Faulkner assigned to them. As noted above, the three monologues show that the brothers are obsessed by their sister Candace in ways which differ from each other in complete accord with the Freudian topographical chart of the divisions of personality. It is in this connection chiefly that we see them suffering because of the phychological bad luck of their family. Benjamin, Id-like, wants Candace, but she is driven entirely away forever. Quentin alternates between wanting Candace and punishing himself for wanting her; and partly because of the failure of his unlucky parents to provide decent psychological support he cannot cope with this conflict as a normally strong Ego might. He acts according to Freudian theory when he seeks punishment from his father by falsely claiming to have committed incest. When his world-weary father will not give him even the support of punishment, Quentin moves to carry out punishment on himself, first considering castration in repetition of that motif of Benjamin's "punishment" but finally deciding upon complete self-destruction by drowning. Jason, Super-ego-like, is in opposition to Benjamin and Candace and therefore to her daughter who is a substitute for her absent mother; but his opposition, gone wildly out of control, becomes frenzy.

The final section of the novel, which follows the three monologues, emphasizes the supportive nature of the Compson's Negro servant Dilsey. She works, while the Compsons do not; she is effectively orderly, while the Compsons are compulsively so; she is in touch with reality and has no interest in making false pretensions. Her presence lets us see the Compson tragedy more clearly, bearing out Quentin's remark that Negroes "come into white people's lives . . . in sudden sharp black trickles that isolate white facts for an instant in unarguable truth like under a microscope."

When Dilsey takes the idiot to her church on Easter in this concluding section of the novel, Faulkner shows us a sample of the love which is missing in the unfortunate Compson family. The minister speaks to the members of the congregation about love until "there was not even a voice but instead their hearts were speaking to one another in chanting measures beyond the need for words." As Dilsey and Benjamin sit in the congregation and Faulkner suggests their similarity to Mary and Jesus, about whom the minister is speaking, we sense a kind of love which the Compsons as a family have not known. The articles on Freudian psychology in *The Encyclopædia Britannica* of 1926 had said:

> The maternal "life reaction" as expressively symbolized by the Madonna and Child, is unfulfilled and incomplete in the majority of women . . . the complete fulfillment . . . is to love, to be loved, to give birth to children and to nourish and cherish them.

The tragedy of the Compsons appears in bold relief in the final scene of the novel. On the last two pages of the book Jason and Benjamin confront each other most violently in an episode which seems to owe its terms and structure to a combination of the *Macbeth* passage discussed at the start of this paper and the Freudian roles which the two brothers play according to the general interpretation of the novel which I have been making. It is a scene of "sound and fury" and illustrates that for these two warped personalities (or parts of a personality) life is "signifying nothing." Benjamin's bellows are described as *sound*, "agony eyeless, tongueless; just sound." And *fury*, in Jason, appears at its peak as we see him "hurling" Luster aside, "slashing" the mare into a plunging gallop as he swings her around to start the carriage toward home, hitting Luster "over the head with his fist," striking Benjamin, breaking the narcissus, ordering Benjamin to "Shut up!" and, in accord with Freud's concept of the Super-ego as censor at the portal, telling Luster, "If you ever cross that gate with him again, I'll kill you." Then, when Jason's furious attack subsides and the carriage begins to move toward the Compson house to take Benjamin back through the gate and behind the "fence" spoken of in the first line of the novel, where Jason now, in the extremity of Super-ego-like repression, will keep him completely confined until he is behind bars forever in the state asylum, Benjamin, soothed by the familiar movement of the carriage and as mercurial in emotion as the Id of Freud's theory, instantly stops bellowing. And his eyes, like the lives to which the Compson family's psychological failures have brought the novel's three interior monologists, are "empty."

Carvel Collins

Miss Quentin's Paternity Again

In a recent article on *The Sound and the Fury*, George R. Stewart and Joseph M. Backus stated, "as a basis for further criticism," that "a very important element of the story" is "the incest between" Caddy and her brother Benjy.[1] Later Mr. Backus published another article which repeats the charge.[2] *The Sound and the Fury* contains evidence which seems to refute this interpretation, and refuting it seems worthwhile for two reasons: First, the novel, which is a fine one, loses some aesthetic significance if Benjy is considered to have copulated with Caddy. Second, a number of readers of Faulkner have accepted this idea that Benjy physically makes love to his sister and have further enlarged the idea to say that Benjy is the father of Miss Quentin

Revised from *Texas Studies in Literature and Language*, II (Autumn 1960). Copyright 1960 by the University of Texas Press. Reprinted by permission of the author and the University of Texas Press.
[1]Stewart and Backus, " 'Each in Its Ordered Place': Structure and Narrative in 'Benjy's Section' of *The Sound and the Fury*," *American Literature*, XXIX (January 1958).
[2]"Names of Characters in Faulkner's *The Sound and the Fury*." *Names*, VI (December 1958).

— an expansion which additionally damages the novel and surely would be artistically repellent to Messrs. Stewart and Backus.

This expansion of the interpretation that Benjy and Caddy are physically lovers makes Benjy the fourth man accused in Miss Quentin's paternity case. Preceding him in the dock have been another of the girl's uncles, Quentin Compson; the traveler, Dalton Ames; and — bewilderingly — the Harvard student, Gerald Bland.

Quentin Compson, the first defendant, was arraigned soon after *The Sound and the Fury* appeared, when readers commonly accepted as true his false confession that he had committed incest with his sister Caddy. Actually, a major point of the novel is that Quentin Compson *is* sexually drawn to his sister; and some critics have missed much of the meaning of the book by taking at face value all the elevated reasons suggested for his suicide. But because of the growth of willingness to read Faulkner's best works with more respect and care, most readers today realize that Quentin Compson does not physically make love to Caddy. So he is fortunately no longer under indictment in his niece's paternity suit.

Unfortunately, however, the three other men have since been charged with fathering Miss Quentin. Seán O'Faoláin tentatively accused two of them in his essay, "William Faulkner: More Genius Than Talent." That Mr. O'Faoláin's essay makes these minor errors — along with several which are much more important — is disheartening. Apparently critics trained in one kind of fiction often are unable, in spite of great perception and sensibility, to convert themselves to sympathy with fiction of a different kind when it comes along. Certainly Mr. O'Faoláin seems in this essay to have been misled in his judgment by a condescension toward Faulkner so extreme that he did not read with serious attention and could write that Miss Quentin "may be the daughter of one Gerald Bland or, more likely, of one Dalton Ames."[3]

It is startling for anyone, even thus tentatively, to make Gerald Bland a defendant in the case. There is no evidence at all that this Harvard student ever even met Caddy. Obviously what led Mr. O'Faoláin astray is the excellent episode at the picnic beside the Charles River when Quentin Compson, caught by reveries in

---

[3] *The Vanishing Hero: Studies in Novelists of the Twenties* (Boston: Little Brown, 1957), p. 94.

the last hours before his suicide, fights Gerald Bland under the delusion he is still fighting Dalton Ames back in Mississippi. Here Quentin Compson and the critic are confused; but William Faulkner is not, nor need the reader be.

Mr. O'Faoláin, though alone in ever having suggested, even tentatively, that Gerald Bland fathered Miss Quentin, is by no means alone when he also suspects Dalton Ames. Examination of the novel, however, disproves the widely held assumption that Dalton Ames is Miss Quentin's father. Ames does make love to Caddy; in fact, he is the first to do so. But the most cursory look at the calendar makes clear that Ames cannot be the father of Miss Quentin.

He first makes love to Caddy in 1909, and it must be in the late spring or the summer because the weather is warm enough for Caddy to sit that evening in the stream near the Compson house and Quentin has not yet left home to start his freshman year at Harvard. Ames does not make love to Caddy over a long period of time, for her mother, suspecting Caddy is having an affair, sets Jason to spy on her. When Mrs. Compson is agitated by Jason's report, her husband suggests that she and Caddy go to French Lick where Caddy may forget Ames (118, 127-128). Mrs. Compson takes Caddy to French Lick, and does so before the end of the summer of 1909 because we read that Quentin Compson is still at home to hear the trunks bumped down the attic stairs (117). When Caddy returns to Jefferson from French Lick she is in such despair over the loss of Ames that she becomes promiscuous (184). The next spring, at her wedding on April 25, 1910, Caddy, pregnant with Miss Quentin, is marrying Herbert Head in order to give the baby a legal father. At the time of this wedding Caddy presumably could have been only a few months pregnant; so she must have conceived Miss Quentin several months after the end of her affair with Dalton Ames, who therefore cannot be Miss Quentin's father.

A major reason many readers incorrectly consider Dalton Ames the father of Miss Quentin is that Quentin Compson thinks obsessively about Ames. This misreading stems from the belief that Quentin Compson's chief concern is his family's honor. But Quentin Compson — who, after all, chiefly cares about himself — actually thinks compulsively about Ames because of personal jealousy, as the scenes by the branch show; and this jealousy is made greater because his sister is, of course, sexually taboo for him. To be the subject of Quentin Compson's driven reveries,

Dalton Ames need not be the father of Caddy's child, he merely need be Caddy's first and most loved lover.

Faulkner seems more responsible for this particular misreading than his critics because several years after the publication of the novel he accepted an assignment to write the semi-expository "Appendix," with its odd statements about Luster and Jason and about Quentin Compson's relationship to Caddy and his concern for honor. The admirable policy of reading any novel by itself without the "aid" of auctorial commentary would seem easy to follow here, because the "Appendix" contains obvious contradictions of several kinds; but much criticism of *The Sound and the Fury* has been marred by the assumption that the "Appendix" is a helpful guide. The damaging effect of the "Appendix" has been increased because of its often having been printed at the beginning of the volume so that many readers have assumed it to be integral with what follows and composed at the same time. This is unfortunate because readers often trust an author's expository remarks about his fiction more than they trust the fiction itself, and the "Appendix" describes a novel inferior to the novel which *The Sound and the Fury* actually is. But in spite of the "Appendix," the novel disproves the contention that Dalton Ames fathered Miss Quentin.

For Benjy to be put forward as another lover of Caddy is in many ways a good corrective to a common misreading of the novel, which has seen Benjy as the "conscience" of the Compson family. Some criticism of this novel even goes so far in this matter as to say that if Benjy's values had prevailed the family might have been saved — a reading which fails to note that such behavior by Benjy as bellowing when Caddy first wears perfume or kisses a boy shows not Benjy's morality but his selfishness and jealousy concerning Caddy, whom he wants to keep to himself. Surely critics cannot believe Faulkner wants us to think perfume and kisses immoral. A good corrective here is to imagine how Benjy would behave if Caddy conventionally fell in love and married and departed with some most admirable man: we can only imagine that Benjy's behavior would be just what it is in the novel as published. The fact that Benjy's "values" — which are concern for himself and disregard for others — actually are those which do "prevail" with most members of his family is precisely why the family is not "saved." By incorrectly holding in high regard the "morality" of the badly treated Benjy, many critics have fallen into the same error critics used to fall into when they regarded Maggie Verver

as an almost wholly admirable person in *The Golden Bowl* because
she is put upon by the adulterers. Victim though Benjy is, he is
selfish in the extreme and only seems moral to readers who overlook that the novel avoids condemning him because he is mentally
below the age of responsibility and consequently is neither moral
nor immoral but amoral. So the reading by Messrs. Stewart and
Backus which holds that Benjy physically makes love to his sister
has done good by helping scotch the idea that he is the conscience
of the family.

But to state that Benjy wants Caddy, as he certainly does, is one
thing and to state that he physically possesses her is quite another
— not borne out by the novel. Messrs. Stewart and Backus state
that "their scrutiny of the developing relationship between Caddy
and Benjy has led them to believe that a very important element
of the story — especially significant in the degradation of the
Compsons — is the incest between the two, most clearly demonstrated in Level L."[4] This level they identify elsewhere in their
article[5] with the episode which they date as "Probably early summer, 1909," when Caddy comes into the house agitated and Benjy
pushes her toward the bathroom (84-85). In the second article, in
Names, Mr. Backus explains further:

> A careful study of the first section of the book, however, strongly
> suggests that Caddy is involved in incest with Benjy. Obviously,
> if Faulkner sought to picture Southern decadence, an incestuous
> affair between his heroine and her idiot brother provides the finish-
> ing touch.[6]

Then the article makes the following additional statement in a
footnote:

> The argument for incest between Caddy and Benjy is based specif-
> ically on such passages as those from the bedroom scene (53) in
> which Dilsey decides it dangerous for Benjy, at 13, to continue
> sleeping with Caddy; the significant bathroom scene (85) in which
> Benjy says he "pushed" at Caddy; and the last scene of Caddy's
> wedding (25) in which Benjy appears to be overpowered by sexual
> frustration. In support of this argument generally, there are Benjy's

---

[4]Stewart and Backus, p. 455*n*.
[5]*Ibid.*, Table II (p. 444).
[6]Backus, pp. 228-229.

increasingly mature desires, his continued dependence upon Caddy, and her consistent willingness to accommodate his needs.[7]

Though Benjy's feelings for Caddy certainly are what we, who use words as Benjy cannot, would call "incestuous," one must point out in passing that on page 25 when Benjy appears to Mr. Backus "to be overpowered by sexual frustration" he is actually vomiting from too much wedding champagne. And one way to avoid many errors in criticism of *The Sound and the Fury* is to drop the assumption that a primary purpose of the novel is "to picture Southern decadence." But the feature of this part of the argument by these two authors is that Benjy copulates with Caddy because Faulkner used the word "pushed" (85) in a subtle way.

Actually the facts about Benjy's "pushing" Caddy would seem to be these: When she is about fourteen years old Caddy puts on perfume. In his primitive, intuitive way — which elsewhere lets him, houndlike, predict the loss of members of the family by death ("He smell hit") — Benjy knows that Caddy's perfume indicates another loss to him: her moving out from his orbit. When Caddy washes away her perfume in the bathroom she has restored herself to Benjy and placated him (48-51). Later, in the second of a progressive series of three carefully related episodes, Caddy has been kissing a boy, and Benjy senses an even greater threat to his relationship with her. When she washes her mouth of the kisses, Benjy is again placated; to him once more "Caddy smelled like trees" (56-58). In the third and climactic related episode — the one which Mr. Backus correctly calls "significant" — Caddy has just come back to the Compson house after losing her virginity to Dalton Ames:

> Caddy came to the door and stood there, looking at Father and Mother. Her eyes flew at me, and away. I began to cry. It went loud and I got up. Caddy came in and stood with her back to the wall, looking at me. I went toward her, crying, and she shrank against the wall and I saw her eyes and I cried louder and pulled at her dress. She put her hands out but I pulled at her dress. Her eyes ran. . . .
>
> We were in the hall. Caddy was still looking at me. Her hand was against her mouth and I saw her eyes and I cried. We went up the stairs. She stopped again, against the wall, looking at me and I cried and she went on and I came on, crying, and she shrank against the

[7] *Ibid.*, pp. 228-229n.

wall, looking at me. She opened the door to her room, but I pulled at her dress and we went to the bathroom and she stood against the door, looking at me. Then she put her arm across her face and I pushed at her, crying. [84-85]

Here Benjy actually would seem merely to be trying once more the old magic of getting rid of competition by forcing Caddy to go to a place where she can wash. But Caddy, knowing that perfume and kissing are one thing and defloration somewhat another, and obviously in considerable agitation over her experience with Dalton Ames, resists Benjy's effort to keep her in their familiar, juvenile relationship. Her increased resistance in this episode and the word "pushed" lead the authors of the two articles to consider Benjy one of Caddy's lovers—and lead others, who go beyond the two articles, to consider Benjy the father of her child.

In the second of the articles Mr. Backus makes a statement which probably explains why perceptive critics could fall into this misreading: "A careful study of the first section of the book . . . strongly suggests that Caddy is involved in incest with Benjy."[8] It is this concentration on the first section of the novel which must have prevented notice of other descriptions of this same episode that appear in the second section, Quentin Compson's monologue. There we learn that after Caddy has been with Ames she comes home to a sitting room containing several members of her family, including her father and mother and her brothers Quentin and Benjy. Benjy intuitively realizes that Caddy has taken a major step sexually away from him:

> . . . *one minute she was standing in the door the next minute he was pulling at her dress and bellowing his voice hammered back and forth between the walls in waves and she shrinking against the wall getting smaller and smaller with her white face her eyes like thumbs dug into it until he pushed her out of the room his voice hammering* [154]

Later Quentin Compson's monologue again describes the scene in a way which seems to refute the idea that in this episode Benjy makes love to Caddy:

> one minute she was standing there the next he was yelling and pulling at her dress they went into the hall and up the stairs yelling

---

[8]*Ibid.*, p. 228.

and shoving at her up the stairs to the bathroom door and stopped her back against the door and her arm across her face yelling and trying to shove her into the bathroom [185]

So, starting in the presence of the family gathered on the first floor of the house, Benjy "pushed" Caddy all the way up the stairs to the bathroom. For the word "pushed" in the novel's first description of this episode to mean that Benjy makes love to Caddy, as has been suggested, we would have to believe what is unlikely if not impossible: that Faulkner intended these later descriptions of the "significant" episode to show us that the Compson family not only condones Benjy's making love to his sister publicly and quite noisily in their assembled presence but that Benjy makes love to her like the hawk of fable — on the wing. It has been a big day for Caddy who has lost her virginity to Dalton Ames; surely critics ask too much of even this concentrated novel that Caddy, a few minutes after returning from her defloration by Ames, should also make love to her bellowing brother in such a public and moving way — and, in the newest extension of the theory, should conceive Miss Quentin by Benjy.

Those who consider Benjy the father of Miss Quentin and believe that he becomes so in this third episode of the *drang nach* water tap confront the same biological contradiction as the proponents of the belief that Dalton Ames is Miss Quentin's father, for human gestation in most fiction requires approximately nine months. Counting on our fingers like village gossips, if we begin at even the very end of the summer of 1909 while Quentin Compson, yet to go to Harvard, is still at home to talk with Caddy about the events of the preceding hours during which she has first made love to Dalton Ames and Benjy has forced her toward the bathroom, we find that if Caddy conceives Miss Quentin that day with either of these candidates the baby's birth at the latest will have to be about the end of May, 1910. That would require Caddy to be eight months pregnant at the time of her wedding to Herbert Head — on whose visual acuity Faulkner casts no aspersion whatever.

So in the search for the father of Miss Quentin it seems likely that the four men so far accused are not guilty: Gerald Bland is not. Dalton Ames is not. Nor is Benjy on that eventful summer day. Statistical examination of fictional parturition in the novel even gives Quentin Compson a solid alibi should he still need it, for he was away at college all year except at Christmas vacation and Caddy's wedding. Who, then, is Miss Quentin's father?

Just before the wedding when Caddy tells her brother Quentin that she is illegitimately pregnant, he asks her, *"Have there been very many Caddy* (142). Caddy, who had lost her virginity to Dalton Ames the previous summer and then almost immediately had lost Dalton Ames himself, replies that there have been *"too many"* (143).

Here and elsewhere in the novel we sense that Caddy's great capacity for love — which makes her care so much for her brothers Benjy and Quentin — is warped by their selfishness and the self-ishness of her parents and is additionally warped into promiscuity by the loss of her first lover, Dalton Ames, the mere sound of whose name can quicken her pulse (203). And though the *"too many"* men with whom she has made love during her discontented winter after the departure of her first lover bear no names in the novel, surely it is one of them who is the father of Miss Quentin.

Miss Quentin's paternity is unknown even to her mother, as Quentin Compson points out (143); and in seeking precisely to identify the man we miss the point. A major subject of this novel is the tragedy caused by the absence of effective love within a family: as one of the Compsons perceptively says, the inadequacies of their selfish parents have *"poisoned"* the Compson children (126). When the novel ends — with Quentin Compson a suicide, Benjy never again to go pleasantly outside the gate, Jason frus-trated by his defeats, and Caddy vanished as a prostitute — it is artistically effective that Miss Quentin, child of the next genera-tion, should be so cut off from familial love that in a sense she has no parents at all. As we watch her disappear into the body politic, we profit aesthetically if we realize that she flees a house where not only has her mother's name been forbidden but her father's name has never even been known.

Eileen Gregory

Caddy Compson's World

"So I, who had never had a sister and was fated to lose my daughter
in infancy, set out to make myself a beautiful and tragic little girl."[1]

Caddy Compson has been inexplicable to most critics of *The
Sound and the Fury,* and it is not easy to focus into a single impression the many fragmented glimpses we are given of her. Catherine
Baum, in a helpful essay, attempts to synthesize the complex data
of Caddy's part in the novel and suggests her role is that of a
central tragic protagonist.[2] Mrs. Baum's is the only full-length

Reprinted by permission of the author
[1]This statement about the conception of *The Sound and the Fury* was made
by William Faulkner in the early 1930's. Michael Millgate, *The Achievement
of William Faulkner* (New York: Random House, 1966), p. 26.
[2]Baum, " 'The Beautiful One': Caddy Compson as Heroine of *The Sound and
the Fury,*" *Modern Fiction Studies,* XIII (Spring 1967), 33-44. Though often
helpful for its full treatment of many aspects of Caddy's character, the essay
is weakened by an excessive dependence on the "Compson Appendix" and by
frequent misreading of the novel on the literal level.

study of Caddy, and, with little exception, other discussions fail
to do justice to the complexity of her character.[3]

One of the major causes of the misinterpretation of Caddy is
the failure of critics to recognize the 1946 "Compson Appendix"
as a piece of writing independent of the 1929 work.[4] A great deal
of caution must be exercised in applying to the original creations
of the novel Faulkner's later analysis of characters. Faulkner's
later description of Caddy in the "Appendix" as "ageless and
beautiful, cold serene and damned"[5] has led many critics astray.
Several directly depend upon the "Appendix" in their analyses of
Caddy. But more frequent among critics is a general prejudice
against Caddy which comes from having read the "Appendix" as
introductory material in the 1946 Modern Library edition and
having assumed it to be an integral part of the novel. Caddy's later
"coldness" and "damnation" are assumed by irresponsible critics

---

[3]In addition to Mrs. Baum's essay, I found the analyses of Caddy's character
by John W. Hunt, *William Faulkner: Art in Theological Tension* (Syracuse:
Syracuse University Press, 1965), and by Walter Brylowski, *Faulkner's
Olympian Laugh: Myth in the Novels* (Detroit: Wayne State University
Press, 1968), to be especially good. Mr. Hunt speaks of Caddy's essential
nature as that of a "matriarch," possessing a natural capacity for love and
compassion. Mr. Brylowski discusses Caddy's role in the "mythic" theme of
innocence and initiation into knowledge of good and evil; and further discusses Caddy's courage and spirit of love as it represents a force of vitality
which is exiled from the Compson family. These essays, along with that of
Brooks, are the best general essays on the novel. In regard to Caddy, I found
less helpful those critics who see her on a wholly naturalistic level. Typical of
the majority of comments about Caddy are those of Olga W. Vickery, *The
Novels of William Faulkner: A Critical Interpretation*, rev. ed. (Baton Rouge:
Louisiana State University Press, 1964), who sees Caddy as "almost a symbol
of the blind forces of nature" (p. 37); Lawrence Bowling, "Faulkner and the
Theme of Innocence," *Kenyon Review*, XX (Summer 1958), who states that
she is "essentially like Jason in that she is a naturalist and never rises above
her natural state" (476); and Michel Gresset, "Psychological Aspects of Evil
in *The Sound and The Fury*," *Mississippi Quarterly*, XIX (Summer 1966),
who feels that she exists "primarily on the level of sensuality" (144). Caddy's
character is certainly more complex than this widespread reading allows for.
[4]Faulkner contributed this piece to the Viking *Portable Faulkner* as the introduction to an excerpt from *The Sound and the Fury* which Malcolm Cowley
wanted to include; it was printed, however, as an independent piece at the end
of the *Portable Faulkner*. In 1946 Random House brought out *The Sound and
the Fury* in a joint volume with *As I Lay Dying* and used the "Compson
Appendix" as a foreword to the novel to replace a proposed introduction
which Faulkner refused to supply. The position of the "Appendix" before the
novel in the 1946 Modern Library edition has caused many readers and critics
to consider Faulkner's later remarks to be an organic part of the novel. James
B. Meriwether, "Notes on the Textual History of *The Sound and the Fury*,"
Papers of the Bibliographical Society of America, LVI (1962), 310-313.
[5]*The Sound and the Fury* (New York: Modern Library, 1965). All subsequent citations from the novel will refer to this edition and will be given in the
body of the paper.

to be present in the Caddy of the novel; such misreading considerably distorts this lovely, passionate young woman.

On the day when their grandmother dies, the Compson children are playing at the branch. Caddy, disobeying a command to come to supper — *"It's not supper time yet. I'm not going"* (19) — squats down in the branch and gets her dress wet. Versh says:

> "Your mommer going to whip you for getting your dress wet."
> "She's not going to do any such thing." Caddy said.
> "How do you know." Quentin said.
> "That's all right how I know." Caddy said. "How do you know."
> "She said she was." Quentin said. [19-20]

Caddy's earliest action in the novel is an act of disobedience; her reaction to the first threat of punishment is a disconcerting self-assurance; Quentin's earliest response to her combines jealousy of her spirit, affirmation of parental authority, and condemnation of the forbidden act. From the beginning Caddy's behavior is unconventional, and her defiance is at odds with the rigid, unnatural moral concern of Quentin — the true heir of his parents' prohibitive and pessimistic moral beliefs. Caddy's potentially tragic character and the nature of her doom are defined in the first part of the novel as she is set in contrast to the other Compsons and the Negroes, whose allegiance to the somewhat shallow convention and morality she cannot accept.

It is essentially an affirmative spirit which causes Caddy to question and to disobey her parents. She is not deliberately perverse in her disobedience but on the contrary is quite simple in her motivation. She decides during the incident at the branch to take off her dress so that it will dry. It is Quentin who makes a moral issue out of this practical gesture, who characteristically insinuates her guilt and antagonism to authority and takes it upon himself to punish her:

> "You just take your dress off." Quentin said. Caddy took her dress off and threw it on the bank. Then she didn't have on anything but her bodice and drawers, and Quentin slapped her and she slipped and fell down in the water. [20-21]

Quentin's motives are complex, childish and transparent though they may be. He is self-righteous, condemning and punishing a forbidden act (undressing); and at the same time he is jealous that Caddy should have the daring to commit the act.

In contrast to Quentin's persistent concern with prohibitions and punishment is Caddy's natural daring. After Quentin and Caddy have fought in the branch and consider the punishment they will receive for being wet, Caddy's instinct is to face up to her punishment directly and immediately, not to evade it. She defies Quentin and Versh's suggestions of secrecy:

> "I bet he [Jason] does tell." Caddy said. "He'll tell Damuddy."
> "He cant tell her." Quentin said. "She's sick. If we walk slow it'll be too dark for them to see."
> "I dont care whether they see or not." Caddy said. "I'm going to tell, myself . . ."
> "Jason wont tell." Quentin said. "You remember that bow and arrow I made you, Jason."
> "It's broke now." Jason said.
> "Let him tell." Caddy said. "I dont give a cuss . . ." [22-23]

After Versh suggested that they slip in the house by the back way, because the "company" might see them, Caddy said:

> "I dont care . . . I'll walk right in the parlor where they are."
> "I bet your pappy whip you if you do." Versh said.
> "I dont care." Caddy said. "I'll walk right in the parlor. I'll walk right in the dining room and eat supper." [26-27]

Caddy's responses at this elementary level help to explain her similar defiance at a later date. She acts not out of a desire for rebellion in itself, but out of a sense of adventure, and in a straightforward and innocent assertion of her will.

Later in the evening, Caddy's curiosity leads her to try to find out about Damuddy's death, although that knowledge has been forbidden to her. Her questions about Damuddy's death and her mother's "sickness" are given evasive answers by her father. And consequently, after Frony has told the children that their grandmother is dead, Caddy cannot comprehend the idea of human death:

> "Dogs are dead." Caddy said, "And when Nancy fell in the ditch and Roskus shot her and the buzzards came and undressed her." [40][6]

---

[6]Caddy continues later, "Do you think buzzards are going to undress Damuddy . . . You're crazy" (42). This association of the "undressing" with death echoes the earlier scene at the branch when Caddy undresses. In Quentin's mind the prohibited act which Caddy commits is associated with the prohibited vision of death.

Caddy deserves and needs an honest and firm explanation of this natural fact; she refuses to allow this secret to be withheld from her and decides to find out what is going on in the house. The relative virtue in her desire for forbidden knowledge is seen in contrast to Quentin's fear of that knowledge. Quentin is older than the other children, and he senses that the crying which they all hear is a sign that something terrible has happened. But his curiosity does not lead him to disobedience. He apparently stays awake, listening to the crying, but makes no attempt to confront the fact of Damuddy's death. Because he accepts the prohibitions of his parents and allows the natural fact of death to remain a terrible secret, he later associates it with the dark horror of Nancy's bones in the matted briers of the ditch;[7] and as a result the forbidden secrets of death and sex become obsessions of Quentin's imagination. Yet Caddy, in assuming the courage to seek "forbidden knowledge," discovers not the horror of death but its normalcy: " 'They're not doing anything in there,' " she says after climbing the tree, " 'Just sitting in chairs and looking' " (55).

Faulkner has stated that the novel grew out of the image of the children looking up into the tree at Caddy's muddy drawers.[8] And this dramatic situation of her "initiation" into knowledge does indeed define something essential about Caddy's tragedy. She should not, after all, have needed to climb the tree; she should have

---

[7]In many instances in the second section, Quentin contemplates his death by water and the resurrection of his bones on Judgment Day: "And I will look down and see my murmuring bones and the deep water like wind, like a roof of wind, and after a long time they cannot distinguish even bones upon the lonely and inviolate sand. Until on the Day when He says Rise only the flat-iron would come floating up" (98); and again, "When you leave a leaf in water a long time after awhile the tissue will be gone and the delicate fibers waving slow as the motion of sleep. They dont touch one another, no matter how knotted up they once were, no matter how close they lay once to the bones. And maybe when He says Rise the eyes will come floating up too . . ." (144). The disintegration of the body into bones is associated in Quentin's mind with Nancy's bones; and his association of death with sex is made clear in the second section in his remembered conversation with Caddy before her rendezvous with Ames. As he and Caddy walk along the path, he is suddenly obsessed with the presence of the ditch (190-191) and finally looks for the bones within it:

lets see if you can still see Nancys bones I havent thought to look in a long time have you
it was matted with vines and briers dark
they were right here you cant tell whether you see them or not can you stop Quentin [191]

[8]Frederick L. Gwynn and Joseph L. Blotner, eds. *Faulkner in the University: Class Conferences at the University of Virginia, 1957-1958* (Charlottesville: University of Virginia Press, 1959), p. 31.

been initiated into the mystery of death in a legitimate way. Yet the unnatural prohibition of her parents, who wish to "protect" their children from the reality of the finite, justifies disobedience. It is Caddy's misfortune that she should be at odds with a moral code which should instruct her in her personal role as a woman, but which, in the feebleness of its authority and in its rigidity, distorts her individual formation. She alone of the children displays the daring to seek initiation into the mystery of forbidden knowledge. Yet in its proper defiance her spirit is fated to suffer for its bravery and forthrightness.

At the time of Damuddy's death, Caddy desires to possess with immediacy what Quentin — by remaining aloof and uninvolved — possesses only in a vague and abstract way: a knowledge of the meaning of death. In a similar manner, Caddy knows instinctively that feminine matriarchal role which Mrs. Compson, in her loveless role-playing, knows only abstractly. Caddy's understanding of Benjy is set against his mother's blindness to his needs. Caddy and her mother are contrasted early in the novel in a scene remembered by Benjy:

> . . . "Come here and kiss Mother, Benjamin."
> Caddy took me to Mother's chair and Mother took my face in her hands and then she held me against her.
> "My poor baby." she said. She let me go. "You and Versh take good care of him, honey."
> "Yessum." Caddy said. We went out . . .
> . . . we stopped in the hall and Caddy knelt and put her arms around me and her cold bright face against mine. She smelled like trees.
> "You're not a poor baby. Are you. You've got your Caddy. Haven't you got your Caddy." [8]

Benjy's attitude is revealed in his inert response to his mother's attention, while he is vividly aware of Caddy's "bright face" and her odor "like trees." Yet beneath Benjy's reactions we see too the contrast between the mother's self-pitying toleration of her "baby" and Caddy's knowledge that Benjy is not "poor" so long as he is loved. She assumes that maternal role of sympathy and care which her mother rejects.

The contrast between Caddy and her mother is again made explicit during Benjy's narration of the events surrounding his rechristening. Mrs. Compson has changed Benjy's name from "Maury" to "Benjamin" because she is ashamed to have him have the name of a Bascomb; and thus she rejects his identity as a child of her flesh and blood. As Benjy and Caddy are sitting peacefully before the fire, Mrs. Compson decides to tell him his new name:

"He's not too heavy." Caddy said. "I can carry him."
"Well, I dont want him carried, then." Mother said. "A five year old child. No, no. Not in my lap. Let him stand up."
"If you'll hold him, he'll stop." Caddy said. "Hush." she said. "You can go right back. Here. Here's your cushion. See."
"Dont, Candace." Mother said.
"Let him look at it and he'll be quiet." Caddy said. ". . . There, Benjy. Look."
I looked at it and hushed.
"You humour him too much." Mother said. "You and your father both. You dont realise that I am the one who has to pay for it . . ."
"You dont need to bother with him." Caddy said. "I like to take care of him. Dont I, Benjy." [77-78]

Mrs. Compson, much as she considers herself a martyr to her children, has never cared enough about Benjy to learn his habits; and, as her actions and words reveal, she blinds herself to the reality of his idiocy — typically — by insisting on a normal and conventional behavior from him. (This attitude and behavior are indeed typical not only of Mrs. Compson but of her sons Quentin and Jason as well.)

Caddy never relinquishes her maternal concern for Benjy, even as she becomes increasingly aware that the world of their childhood is doomed to be destroyed. Benjy narrates a series of memories which involve Caddy's increasing maturity — events which foreshadow and threaten the eventual loss of Caddy as the center of his existence. The reader should not accept Benjy's grief as a condemnation of Caddy. She understands his sorrow and jealousy, as, in her growing knowledge of the world, she is more and more touched with the world's impurity. Benjy bellows in reaction to any sign of disorder in his universe. When Caddy wears perfume, and the odor of trees[9] — which he associates with her very being — is gone, his world is threatened with chaos; when he sees her kissing a boy he senses that Caddy's affection is directed away from the confines of the family. In these instances, and in the painful encounter with Benjy after the loss of her

---

[9]Brylowski, pp. 60ff., discusses the significance of Caddy's identification with trees to signify her virginity and Edenic innocence.

virginity, Caddy's grief stems not so much from a sense of shame over her lost innocence as from her awareness that Benjy's happiness must eventually be destroyed. Change is inevitable, and she must grow up while Benjy is doomed to remain three years old.

The courageous and compassionate young girl who is revealed in Benjy's section is the same character who is victim of the shadowy tragedy narrated by Quentin in the second part. Caddy instinctively possesses a virginal purity and a passionate spirit. But her vitality is threatened by Mrs. Compson in her exaltation of a rigid code of "honor," a falsified Cult of the Lady, and by Mr. Compson in an excessive Calvinism, a Manichean disgust for woman's body as a vessel of corruption. Caddy's strength is that she senses the truth of her femininity and can resist the intimidation of a moral code which would have her remain passive and innocent of finite experience. She realizes that "virginity" and "honor," at least as she has been poorly taught the words by her parents, are merely prohibitive signs used to avoid an acceptance of the finite reality of the body. She acts upon her instinctive knowledge that whatever "honor" exists lies not in obedience to a rigid code, but in a selfless and innocent exercise of the spirit. And her tragic situation, which she recognizes quite early in her life, is that there is no place for her in her family. Nor, unfortunately, is there any place at all for her outside its limits — in the secular world to which she finally resigns herself.

Caddy's doom is instrumented by two men — Dalton Ames and her brother Quentin — and brought to completion by a third — Herbert Head — each of whom misunderstands and destroys the precious reality of her courage and femininity. Ames, to whom she willingly gives her virginity, possesses a debased and cynical vision of woman.[10] Almost blind to her worth, he ultimately causes Caddy to believe that she is worthless. Quentin, her lover by a kind of spiritual incest, attacks her with his moralistic and artificial concepts of virtue and his Calvinistic disgust with fleshly corruption, and urges her to accept guilt for her "lost honor." And in her despair after the loss of Ames, she surrenders to him. Finally, her marriage to Herbert Head symbolically completes and defines her personal destruction.

We know very little about Dalton Ames. He obviously possesses great vitality and masculinity. To Caddy he is also the possesser

---

[10]His brutal cynicism in the belief that all women are "bitches" is echoed later in the novel by Jason's credo, "Once a bitch always a bitch" (223).

of knowledge, having experienced a world more mysterious and grand than hers; she tells Quentin that "he's crossed all the oceans all around the world" (187). Caddy is attracted to him, as Mrs. Baum has noted, with the innocence and awe of a Desdemona.[11] Her self-abandon in the passion of her love is a response to that quality in Dalton which she most needs. Caddy's tragic situation is that she must exercise her selfless love for Dalton outside the sanction of law and convention. She defies her family's moral code in her love for him because his ethic demands that their relationship have no permanence or orthodox foundation. She breaks all bonds of allegiance to her family and yet receives no bond of constancy from him. Caddy is abandoned by Dalton; in his crass, brutal masculinity, his belief that all women are "bitches" (199), he denies the purity of Caddy's femininity and the worth of her love.

Ames' cynicism and casual attitude toward his affair with Caddy are made explicit in his dialogue with Quentin when he comes to revenge his sister's "lost honor." When Quentin first sees Ames, he has "a piece of bark in his hands breaking pieces from it and dropping them over the rail into the water" (197). The bark which Ames shreds and drops into the river echoes Benjy's association of Caddy with "trees"; and it is therefore significant that Ames, throughout his conversation with Quentin, continues to destroy the bark, breaking it, dropping it into the water and watching it float away. In a further extension of the symbolic meaning of the bark, Ames, after Quentin has attempted to fight him, demonstrates his "masculine" skill with a pistol:

> he took the bark from the rail and dropped it into the water it bobbed up the current took it floated away his hand lay on the rail holding the pistol loosely we waited
> you cant hit it now
> no
> it floated on it was quite still in the woods I heard the bird again and the water afterward the pistol came up he didnt aim at all the bark disappeared then pieces of it floated up spreading he hit two more of them pieces of bark no bigger than silver dollars [199]

It is a tragic misfortune that Caddy's genuine and full love should be yielded to one who can only waste it. Yet Ames' desertion of her is only part of Caddy's drama. She is also betrayed

---

[11]Baum, 39.

by Quentin and his distorted sense of morality. From our first glimpse of him as a child it is evident that Quentin is abnormally sensitive to the prohibitions which are given to the children and is obsessively concerned with the punishment and guilt which result from disobedience. He has inherited his parents' Calvinism, which frustrates his desire to partake of the "forbidden" knowledge of sex and death. His incestuous attraction toward Caddy comes in part from an instinctive desire to possess her spirit — the innocent courage which causes her to taste of forbidden knowledge — as his own; yet at the same time that he covets her courage and her knowledge, he fears and recoils from the reality of fleshly experience. Ultimately he seeks to break Caddy's spirit by forcing upon her the sense of guilt which rules his own action.[12] The conversations between Caddy and Quentin — the most dramatically intense dialogues in Faulkner's fiction — reveal Caddy's gradual acceptance of Quentin's possessive will. As Caddy begins to doubt her worth as a woman through Ames' rejection of her, Quentin in his metaphysical jealousy attempts to make her accept blame for her sin, to think of her femininity not as the positive and innocent reality which it is, but as a contemptible and corrupt promiscuity.

Quentin's attitude toward Caddy is selfish and perverted, and it is his impurity of mind, his obsession with the obscenity of sex and his secret desire for it — and not an impurity on Caddy's part — which is revealed through his remarks. In their earlier conversation, after Quentin has realized that she has lost her virginity, the passion of Caddy's tragedy is revealed through the coloring veil of Quentin's vision. Her affair with Dalton Ames is obviously coming to a close; when she meets him later that night she feels compelled to apologize and tells him that "you dont have to if you dont want to" (192). The vitality of their passion has passed, and Caddy is beginning to know the loneliness of abandonment. She is at the branch, lying in the water, when Quentin sees her. She has sacrificed a great deal to a man who does not value her love; and in a grief and dread which she has not yet consciously acknowledged, she begins to feel the impurity of having been exploited, violated — not simply physically, but spiritually violated — by him. And without the strength of Dalton's love to support her, her family's condemnation of her actions

---

[12]John W. Hunt, p. 57, discusses Quentin's reaction to Caddy in great detail and likewise sees Quentin as the agent of Caddy's final destruction.

also has its effect. Lying in the water of the branch she reveals her sense of uncleanliness, symbolically desiring to be cleansed of her now irredeemable "fall."

In the conversation and the events of the evening Quentin attempts to force his moral will upon Caddy, and she, in her sense of despair in her doomed love for Ames, is passive and receptive to him. Quentin's real desire in the encounter is to have Caddy admit that she hates Ames and despises the taste of sexual knowledge which she has stolen:

> Caddy you hate him dont you
> she moved my hand up against her throat her heart was hammer-
> ing there
> poor Quentin
>
>   .   .   .
>
> yes I hate him I would die for him I've already died for him I die
> for him over and over again everytime this goes [187-188]

Caddy is kind to Quentin, who she realizes is pathetic, though she still expresses the passion and devotion with which she has given herself to Ames. However, her reiteration that she would "die" for him, that she dies for him at every heartbeat, reveals her growing sense of despair at her loss and her tragic awareness of the pain with which she tried to purchase his love.

Quentin's obsession with the broken taboo of Caddy's virginity compels him to attempt a ritualistic murder with his knife:

> it wont take but a second Ill try not to hurt
> all right
> will you close your eyes
> no like this youll have to push it harder
> touch your hand to it
> but she didnt move her eyes were wide open looking past my head
> at the sky
> Caddy do you remember how Dilsey fussed at you because your
> drawers were muddy
> dont cry
> Im not crying Caddy
> push it are you going to
> do you want me to
> yes push it
> touch your hand to it
> dont cry poor Quentin [189]

One of the primary reasons for Quentin's action is simply that he wishes for Caddy to admit by her compliance to his will that her sin is heinous enough to deserve death; he assumes the role of executioner in behalf of the abstract moral code by which she stands irrevocably condemned. For this reason he subconsciously associates this present moment with a similar incident on the day when Damuddy died: Caddy's transgression of her parents' command, and Quentin's punishment of her in an act of violence. Yet too, in proposing a double suicide Quentin desires that Caddy surrender to his will irrevocably, that they be united in a single, self-destructive act. Caddy does surrender. She accepts the implicit condemnation of Quentin's code and his act of symbolic possession. Even though she probably knows that Quentin does not have the courage to kill her, she nevertheless does choose — in acceptance of her doom — to yield to his despair.

Caddy the innocent woman becomes promiscuous after this event not simply because she has lost her virginity, or because Dalton Ames has deserted her, but because she has in despair accepted Quentin's suggestion that her femininity is corrupt at the source: she tells Quentin, at the close of her affair with Dalton Ames, "Im bad anyway you cant help it" (196), fatalistically acknowledging her precious womanhood to be corrupt and damned. Her destruction is symbolically completed in her marriage to Herbert Head, whose character expresses all that is most contemptible and base in the secular world to which Caddy has resigned herself. He is indeed a "blackguard" who is garishly materialistic and boorish, whose only concerns are money and sex. Caddy's union with him seems as incongruous and wrong as Eula Varner's marriage to Flem Snopes in Faulkner's later novel *The Hamlet*. Yet it is Caddy herself who has chosen Herbert Head; Caddy who has tragically put aside her self-esteem to signify formally that she is as worthless as he is.

As Caddy talks to Quentin before her marriage, she reveals the nature of the doomed existence which she has willfully chosen to live. She has been living a life of the flesh, and yet feels a sense of uncleanliness — as she orders Quentin repeatedly,"*Dont touch me dont touch me*" (139) — and a sense of guilt for the sin of the flesh which she repeatedly enacts. It does not seem that she has received pleasure from her illegitimate affairs, but rather a grotesque sense of horror:

There was something terrible in me sometimes at night I could see it through them grinning at me through their faces . . .

It is the death's head, the image of the end of fleshly existence, which looks at her "through their faces." Her sense of a profound void in her life — her terrible vision of living death — is associated with her affair with Ames and its aftermath; for she tells Quentin: *"I died last year I told you I had but I didnt know then what I meant"* (153). Ames and Quentin together have effected her spiritual death. Her acceptance of irredeemable guilt, her self-condemnation, has killed a precious part of her; and in sexual experience she perpetually reenacts that self-condemnation and guilt and is haunted by a sense of dread and a fear of damnation. Living a fleshly existence she suffers a continual death through the flesh.

In the Wasteland of *The Sound and the Fury*, Caddy Compson cannot fulfill her natural feminine role. Her tragedy, like that of Emma Bovary and Anna Karenina, is that her fine spirit and femininity are doomed to be victimized and destroyed. Her world is one in which there is no man worthy of her — a brutalized, secular world, in which her great spiritual vitality and capacity for love are spoiled and wasted.

John V. Hagopian

Nihilism in Faulkner's
The Sound and the Fury

Immediately upon the publication of *The Sound and the Fury* in 1929, Evelyn Scott asserted that Dilsey, the compassionate and enduring Negro servant of the degenerate Compson family, was to be taken as the moral norm of the novel. "Dilsey," she said, "provides the beauty of coherence against the background of struggling choice. She recovers for us the spirit of tragedy which the patter of cynicism has often made seem lost."[1] Twenty years later Sumner C. Powell called attention to the Christian dimensions of Dilsey's values, citing Faulkner's "use of the Christian order as a dramatic contrast to the disorder of the Compsons and as a judgment on them."[2] Soon after that, Faulkner's Nobel Prize Speech of 1950 stimulated a decade of critiques which interpret Dilsey as the moral norm, thereby making *The Sound and the Fury* a novel which embodies some positive moral vision,

From *Modern Fiction Studies*, XIII (Spring 1967), pp. 45-55. Reprinted by permission the Purdue Research Foundation.
[1]Quoted with apparent approval by William Van O'Connor, *The Tangled Fire of William Faulkner* (Minneapolis: University of Minnesota Press, 1954), p. 44.
[2]"William Faulkner Celebrates Easter, 1928," *Perspective*, II (1949), 215.

often denoted as Christian.[3] That view remained almost without serious challenge until Cleanth Brooks recently asserted that "The title of *The Sound and the Fury* . . . provides a true key, for the novel has to do with the discovery that life has no meaning." Brooks conceded that "For Dilsey life does have meaning . . . [but] Faulkner makes no claim for Dilsey's version of Christianity one way or the other. His presentation of it is moving and credible, but moving and credible as an aspect of Dilsey's own mental and emotional life."[4] However, if Brooks is correct that the title *is* an accurate indication that "the novel has to do with the discovery that life has no meaning," then Faulkner does make a claim against Dilsey's version of Christianity — for the novel itself denies it. Furthermore, Brooks does not show how the structure, especially that of the so-called Dilsey section, supports the notion that the title is indeed an accurate guide to the meaning. It is the burden of this paper to demonstrate that a structural analysis of the closing chapter of *The Sound and the Fury* does, in fact, reveal nihilism as the meaning of the whole.

---

[3]A sampling of opinions in the full-length studies confirms this. Irving Howe: "Dilsey [is] strong, whole, uncorrupted. She is the voice of judgment over the Compsons and their world." *William Faulkner: A Critical Study* (New York: Random House, 1952), p. 41; Hyatt Waggoner: "[Dilsey is] a kind of foster-mother of Christ, the enabling agent of revelation at once spiritual and aesthetic." *William Faulkner: From Jefferson to the World* (Lexington: University of Kentucky Press, 1959), p. 46; Walter J. Slatoff: "[The final scene of Benjy and Luster] does not negate the moderate affirmation of the Dilsey episode, nor does it really qualify it. Rather it stands in suspension with it as a commentary of equal force." *Quest for Failure* (Ithaca, New York: Cornell University Press, 1960), p. 157; Olga Vickery: "Dilsey . . . becomes through her actions alone the embodiment of the truth of the heart which is synonymous with morality. . . . In a sense, Dilsey represents a final perspective directed toward the past and the Compsons, but it is also the reader's perspective for which Dilsey merely provides the vantage point. . . ./There is no doubt but that Dilsey is meant to represent the ethical norm, the realizing and acting out of one's humanity." *The Novels of William Faulkner* (Baton Rouge: Louisiana State University Press, 1959), pp. 32, 47; Michael Millgate: "Faulkner's main concern in this [final] section is apparently to establish firm images of order, stability, and trust to set over against the images of disorder, decay, selfishness, and deceit which have dominated the earlier sections." *William Faulkner* (Edinburgh: Oliver and Boyd, 1961), p. 32; F. J. Hoffman: "Faulkner associates her [Dilsey's] dignity and power of endurance with universal truths and values, which will become the final means of judging the Compsons. . . . / From these several objective portraits [in the last chapter] it becomes obvious that the one of Dilsey will dominate and that in its terms Faulkner intends a final perspective upon the Compson story." *William Faulkner* (New York: Twayne, 1961), pp. 58-59.
[4]*William Faulkner: The Yoknapatawpha County* (New Haven: Yale University Press, 1963), pp. 347, 348.

More than fifteen years ago Mark Schorer explained that technique is the only means that a writer has of "discovering, exploring, developing his subject, of conveying its meaning, and, finally, of evaluating it."[5] *The Sound and the Fury* has, unfortunately, been too often discussed in terms of readers' responses to various individual characters, or of Faulkner's latter-day reminiscences and philosophizing, or of the morality of Southern Protestantism, rather than in terms of technique. One of the most crucial elements of technique is closure, namely, the means by which the action is rounded off and rendered whole and the meaning finally embodied;[6] and an analysis of closure is one of the most economical ways of reaching an understanding of the total form of a work. What has hitherto not been observed of the final chapter of *The Sound and the Fury* is that it has four parts: a prologue, and three distinct actions which develop motifs that are first struck in the prologue. Furthermore, each of the final three movements recapitulates themes and motifs of the first three chapters — the Quentin, Jason, and Benjy sections, respectively — and each ends on a semblance of closure. However, the first two of these closures are merely tentative. They are false conclusions, and in proceeding beyond them Faulkner is, in effect, repudiating the terms by which they would have determined the total form-content. The final closure encapsules everything that precedes it and shapes the ultimate meaning of the novel.

Perhaps two schematic summaries will serve to clarify these general ideas before they are explored in detail.

I.

STRUCTURE OF THE FINAL CHAPTER

Prologue
Dawn to 9:30 a.m.
All remaining Compsons and Gib-

---

[5]"Technique and Discovery," *Hudson Review*, I (Spring 1948), 67.
[6]Students of Gestalt psychology will recognize that I am using a variation of a technical term in that discipline. *Closure* is, of course, not a synonym of *conclusion*. *Closure* is determined by the internally unifying force or set of vector forces that structure an object and render it as a meaningful, discreet, and perceptible whole. However, such a whole—even a work of literature—need not have a conclusion to be "closed;" *vide* a circle or Joyce's *Finnegans Wake*. Although *The Sound and the Fury* shares with *Finnegans Wake* the feature of having the ending lead in some way back to the opening, it does not as literally make a circle of the work. Only thematically does Faulkner's ending recapitulate the opening. *The Sound and the Fury* does have a conclusion, and as in most novels its conclusion provides important elements of closure.

sons at home; three movements
toward closure foreshadowed

1.	2.
Movement to	*Movement to*
Tragic-Christian Closure	*Socio-Economic Closure*
9:30 a.m. to 1:30 p.m.	9:30 a.m. to 1:30 p.m.
Dilsey's stately walk to church	Jason's furious drive to the carni-
and return—a recapitulation of	val in pursuit of Miss Quentin—a
the theme of Quentin section	recapitulation of the theme of
	Jason section

3.

Movement to Nihilistic Closure
1:30 to about 3 p.m.
Benjy and Luster's erratic trip by horse and buggy to monument—
a recapitulation of the theme of the Benjy section

II.
RELATION OF THE THREE CLOSURES TO THE
ENTIRE NOVEL

Chapter 1:	*Chapter 2:*	*Chapter 3:*
Benjy	Quentin	Jason
Nihilism	Christian Morality	Socio-Economic
	[Bracketed by Mr. Comp-	values
	son's nihilistic philosophy]	

Chapter 4:

First Closure
casts novel in
Tragic-Christian terms

Second Closure
casts novel in
Socio-economic terms

Third Closure
casts novel in
Nihilistic Existential terms

I. STRUCTURE OF THE FINAL CHAPTER

Prologue: Dawn to 9:30 a.m. (pp. 330-359)[7]

In moving from ritual to rage to irrationality, the opening section of the last chapter focuses first on Dilsey (330-345), then on

---

[7]In the quotations from *The Sound and the Fury* which follow, all italics are
mine.

Jason (345-354), and finally on Benjy and Luster (354-359) in a thematic progression that foreshadows the three closure movements which follow. That Dilsey's values cannot prevail is seen immediately in the symbolism that marks her first emergence from the cabin. Dilsey appears dressed in "colour regal and moribund," the theological purple of her silk dress covered by the royal maroon of her velvet cape. But that cape has a "border of mangy and anonymous fur" which significantly undermines the symbolic power of those colors. Indeed, Faulkner tells us that "the days or the years had consumed" Dilsey's strength, leaving only a "ruin." As Dilsey completes her stately ritual of emergence and withdrawal, "A pair of jaybirds came up from nowhere, . . . swung in raucous tilt and recover, screaming into the wind that ripped their harsh cries . . ." (331-332). That their cries are a sardonic mockery of all Dilsey stands for is suggested shortly afterward when Luster throws a rock at the jaybirds, shouting, "Git on back to hell, whar you belong at. 'Taint Monday yit" (335). Thus hellish forces invade the peace and calm of a cold Easter morning, signifying that Christian values cannot appease or redeem the meaningless violence of the Compsons. Then when Dilsey, dressed in blue gingham (the Virgin's color) re-emerges from her cabin and enters the house, she hears the whining of Mrs. Compson, who is dressed in "a dressing gown of quilted black satin" (Satan's color). Dilsey can patiently endure the Compsons, but cannot prevail over them. Arbitrarily summoned by Mrs. Compson's demand that she dress Benjy and then halted half-way up the stairs by the contradictory demand that she immediately prepare Jason's breakfast, Dilsey stops "With her foot lifted to the next step . . . her hand against the wall . . . motionless and shapeless" (338). Dilsey's gesture of appeasement is paralyzed and she returns to her kitchen. Restored to her proper domain, Dilsey resumes singing as she works, "something without particular tune or words, repetitive, mournful and plaintive, austere" (336). Indeed, she is the only character in the novel who orders and expresses her experience in song, but it is not a song of triumph and no one listens or learns from her. When the kitchen clock strikes five times, Dilsey can confidently announce that it is eight o'clock, but she cannot set the Compson clock in order. And, as she listens, there is "no sound save the clock *and the fire*" (342). Finally, in control of the instruments of ritual order, she rings "a small clear bell" summoning the Compsons to breakfast; but when Jason arrives, he introduces the second motif of the prologue — disorder and, in his behavior to follow, a mockery of the rituals of Easter.

It is now Jason, and not Dilsey, who dominates the scene with his fury at the broken window in his room and at Miss Quentin's absence from the breakfast table. He commands Dilsey to summon her — a command Dilsey cannot fulfill. Mrs. Compson apologizes to Jason for having given the Negroes permission to attend church, and Jason deliberately misunderstands her to mean the carnival. This is only one of a series of gratuitous insults to Christian institutions, and a foreshadowing of the church and carnival episodes which immediately follow the prologue. Upon his discovery that Miss Quentin has run off with the money, Jason becomes a Snopesish "man in motion," accompanied by the swirl of jaybirds shrieking past the house. His frantic gestures are in strong contrast with the ritual dignity and grace of Dilsey at the opening of the prologue.

With Jason gone, the focus shifts to Benjy and Luster, and the emphasis is on the motif of Benjy's "slow bellowing sound, *meaningless and sustained*" (356). It is the subsequent development of this motif that finally closes the novel. Before taking Benjy to the pasture, Luster comically underlines the fact that Benjy is a manifestation of meaninglessness when he protests to Dilsey, "I aint lyin. Ask Benjy ef I is" (357). Benjy can never affirm or deny anything; he can only be, and his being is nothingness.

The First Two Movements Toward Tentative Closures 9:30 a.m. to 1:30 p.m.

1. *Dilsey to and from the Church* (pp. 358-376)
2. *Jason to and from the Carnival* (pp. 376-392)

These two actions function as a kind of dissonant counterpoint. The morning bells of the church mark Dilsey's second stately emergence from her cabin, dressed once again in the symbolic theological and royal colors (358), and the same bells also mark Jason's frenzied drive to the sheriff's house (376). Both are mocked by Benjy's "hopeless and prolonged" wail, "all time and injustice and sorrow become vocal for an instant by a conjunction of planets" (359). That wail suggests the futility both of Dilsey's rituals to order the chaos of the universe and of Jason's attempts to recover his money. As she moves through a wasteland landscape toward church, Dilsey exchanges ritual greetings with the other communicants — "Sis' Gibson! How you dis mawnin?" / "I'm well. Is you well?" / "I'm right well, I thank you" (363); at the same time Jason rejects the sheriff's greeting with a peremptory "You ready to go now?" (376). The Negroes move toward church "with slow sabbath deliberation" (364), while Jason drives "on out of the bells and out of town" thinking "every damn one of them will be at church" (381). The members of the Negro congregation are attuned to their God and drawn "to one another in chanting measures beyond the need for words" (367), but Jason imagines himself (like Satan in *Paradise Lost*, VI: 135) "dragging Omnipotence down from His throne, if necessary; of the embattled legions of both hell and heaven through which he tore his way and put his hands at last on his fleeing niece" (382). As Reverend Shegog greets his "Breddren en sistuhn" (368), Jason erupts into the pullman car of the carnival with an imperious "Where are they? . . . Quick, now" (386) and becomes involved in a furious battle with the indignant carnival hands (386-388). At that very moment the minister is preaching about "de angels singin de peaceful songs en de glory" (369). As the sermon closes with a reference to "de arisen dead whut got de blood en de ricklickshun of de Lamb" (370), Jason is "falling, thinking So this is how it'll end, and he believed that he was about to die" (387). On the next page is a drawing of the electric eye of Mottson looking down on Jason, an eye surely derived from the degenerate technological god manifested by Fitzgerald's Dr. T. J. Eckleburg in *The Great Gatsby*. By 12:30 both the church service and Jason's pursuit are ended. Back in the house, Dilsey enters a "pervading reek of camphor" in Mrs. Compson's room (373), just as Jason in terrible pain from his headache thinks "I can get something [camphor] for it at Jefferson" (391). At one o'clock, having summoned Luster and Benjy to dinner, Dilsey repeats, "Jason aint comin home" (375, 376) at the same moment that Jason "wasn't thinking of home, where Ben and Luster were eating cold dinner at the kitchen table. Something . . . permitted him to forget Jefferson as any place which he had ever seen before, where his life must resume itself" (392).

Although these two extended passages are stretched over exactly the same time period and embody a thematic contrast in a considerable number of details, each independently constitutes a different movement toward closure. The focus on Dilsey comes first and presents only the first of three possible conclusions for the novel as a whole. "I've seed de first en de last," says Dilsey — and "I seed de beginnin, en now I sees de endin" (371). These pronouncements, together with the return from church to the "square, paintless house with its rotting portico" (372), would have terminated the novel in such a way as to make of the Reverend Shegog's sermon an appropriate epigraph for the entire novel. The completed action would then be seen from a Christian perspective, for, indeed, "de generations passed away," and the Compson line, which "aint got de milk en de dew of de old salvation" (368, 369), has come to an end.

The idea that Christian values cannot redeem the Compsons was already dramatized in Chapter II when Quentin, unable to prove false his father's nihilistic pronouncements, committed suicide. In the first closure of the last chapter the same idea is recapitulated by Dilsey, who realizes that the Compson line comes to an end without salvation. Just as surely as Quentin's watch without hands, Dilsey's broken kitchen clock confirms Mr. Compson's observation that "Christ was not crucified: he was worn away by a minute clicking of little wheels" (94). The irony of Dilsey's faith in the Christian message of Reverend Shegog — just like the irony of her certainty that she can see through the disorder of time — was foreshadowed in the Quentin section when Quentin recalled that a brothel full of Negroes in Memphis "went into a religious trance ran naked into the street. It took three policemen to subdue one of them. Yes Jesus O good man Jesus O that good man" (212). At Dilsey's Easter service a member of the congregation had chanted, "I sees, O Jesus! Oh I sees!" (370).

But Faulkner abandons this Christian motif and for the second ending shifts the focus to Jason's futile pursuit of his niece and his money. This recapitulates Chapter III, "April Sixth 1928," when once before Jason pursued his niece in a pain-wracked drive through the countryside around Jefferson. It is significant, too, that his departure and return in a power-driven machine, symbolic of the money-drives of the industrial age, contrasts with the slow, deliberate pace of the Negroes moving on foot to church

and back. Accompanying this contrast is a contrast in tone between the tragic and the sardonic-comic. Jason is almost reduced
to the level of a Tom and Jerry cartoon and the action closes
with the frustrated Jason hoist with his own petard as the Negro
charges him four dollars to drive him back to Jefferson. Here,
too, the novel might have ended without the least suggestion of
seeming incomplete. The final perspective would then have been
a socio-economic one, evoking the "thirty pieces of silver" rather
than the milk and the dew of the old salvation. Had that been
the case *The Sound and the Fury* would have required consideration as an exposé of the anti-Christian materialism of the New
South, similar to that of the comic Snopes trilogy.

Final Conclusion: 1:30 to about 3 p.m.

3. *Luster and Benjy's Abortive Progress* (392-401)

As Faulkner moves beyond the two closures described above,
he shifts perspective to the action of Luster and Benjy. This
thematically takes us back full circle to the opening of the novel,
where neither God nor Mammon prevails — merely chaos and
meaninglessness. Once again Benjy moans before his stalk of
jimson weed; once again he howls at the golfers' calls for "Caddie";
and once again he finds only temporary solace in Dilsey's compassion for him.

It becomes clear to Dilsey that Benjy cannot remain quiet
until four o'clock when T. P. is to drive him to the cemetery, and
she reluctantly lets Luster take him. This time the movement
away from the house is neither on foot or by machine — it is by
animal. The aged mare Queenie is hitched to a broken-down
surrey; her gait is slow, but hardly dignified — "resembling a prolonged and suspended fall" (398). Moving in the direction of
death (i.e., the cemetery), Benjy's eyes are as empty as those
of the statue of the Confederate soldier, until his purely meaningless sense of order is violated when Luster swings the horse
to the left of the monument. Then "Bellow on bellow" Benjy's
voice mounts, until Jason leaps on the surrey, strikes both Luster
and Benjy, and whips the horse into a plunging gallop homeward.
"Benjy, fer God's sake!" shouts Luster, invoking the Deity for
the first time — and in vain. Finally, "his [Ben's] eyes were empty
and blue and serene again as cornice and façade flowed smoothly

once more from left to right; post and tree, window and doorway, and signboard, each in its ordered place" (401).

Thus the novel reaches its final closure in heavily ironic terms: Jason, his paradise lost, vents his violence not to drag Omnipotence down from His throne, but for purely selfish motives to restore a meaningless sense of order. It is reminiscent of the end of Chapter I when after another very hard day for Benjy, "the dark began to go in smooth, bright shapes, like it always does, even when Caddy says that I have been asleep" (92). At the end, for the first time in the novel, Faulkner does not bring the action from dawn to darkness; instead he thematically bends the novel back to its beginning. The terms of closure are neither Christian nor socio-economic; they are nihilistic. It is the *reducto absurdum* of the experience of Easter Sunday and the Easter week-end.

II. RELATION OF CLOSURE TO THE BODY OF THE NOVEL

Faulkner himself has said that in the last chapter he "tried to gather the pieces together and fill in the gaps by making [himself] the spokesman."[8] The first three chapters are presented from the perspective of the three Compson brothers, each with his own peculiarly distorted sense of time. Benjy's view is that of the eternal present. He has no awareness of the past as past; fragments of past events occur to him in an achronological sequence, all as if they were occurring on April 7, 1928. Quentin, on the other hand, is past-oriented — even past-obsessed. He associates almost all present events with episodes of the past, or sees the present itself as inevitably becoming the past. In committing suicide, he enacts his father's dictum that "its not even time until it was" (222). Jason, however, is a "man in motion" constantly projecting himself into the future, scrambling out of the past and the present as fast as he can into future wealth, power, and status: "just let me have twenty-four hours without any damn New York jew to advise me. . . . once I've done that they can bring all Beale Street and all bedlam in here" (329). None of the Compson

---

[8]James B. Meriwether and Michael Millgate, eds., *Lion in the Garden: Interviews with William Faulkner, 1926-1962* (New York: Random House, 1968), p. 245.

brothers lives in harmony with an orderly rhythm of time. Nevertheless, all their time-perspectives have in common that necessary attribute of any stream-of-consciousness — the experiencing of all present events in an irreversible, one-directional flow. Each of the first three chapters moves inexorably from morning to night, however much that movement is broken by flash-forwards, flash-backs, or memories.[9]

However, when Faulkner shifts in the last chapter from the subjective points-of-view of his characters to an objective narrator's perspective, he is no longer bound to any one character's sense of time. Hence, it is inaccurate to say, as Cleanth Brooks does, that "It is only in the fourth section of the book, the one dominated by Dilsey, that we enter into a proper notion of time."[10] To be sure, the flow of present time is not interrupted by any recapitulation of events from the past, yet neither does it move in an irreversible, one-directional flow. Nor is the focus solely on Dilsey. As we have seen, the prologue shifts from character to character before the narrator temporarily fixes on Dilsey's progression to and from the Easter services — an action that moves from 9:30 to 1:30. But then, for the first time in the novel, the forward motion of time is broken off and those same four hours are presented in terms of Jason's actions. When the time sequence again reaches 1:30, the narrator focuses attention on Benjy and Luster until the climatic events at the Confederate monument in mid-afternoon. Since there are, after the prologue, three time sequences each focused on a different character or characters, it is simply false to assert that the last chapter embodies either Dilsey's point-of-view or her notion of time.

Although the objective narrator manipulates the time-flow of the last chapter, he does so to deal with themes that were presented from the purely subjective points-of-view of the earlier chapters. And thus he makes objective and authorial the futility of Christian values to order the Compson experience in terms of sin and redemption. Faulkner's chorus figure is Quentin's father, Jason Compson III. The father's nihilistic pronouncements open and close the Quentin section. At the beginning Quentin recalls him saying, "[in this watch] I give you the mausoleum of all

---

[9]A flashback may be defined as an interruption of present events with a past event which is consciously experienced by the character as *past*; but a flash-forward is an interruption of present events by a past event which is consciously experienced by the character as a *present* event.
[10]Brooks, p. 328.

hope and desire . . . the reducto absurdum of all human experience. . . . Because no battle is ever won. . . . They are not even
fought. The field only reveals to man his own folly and despair,
and victory is an illusion of philosophers and fools. . . . / . . .
nothing is even worth the changing of it" (93, 96). At the end
he is remembered saying, "a love or a sorrow is a bond purchased
without design. . . . / [temporary] was the saddest word of all
there is nothing else in the world its not despair until time its
not even time until it was" (221, 222). The action of his three
sons and of the novel as a whole confirms Mr. Compson. It is
because Quentin realizes that his father is right, that it is futile
to look to Jesus and St. Francis for any meaningful guide to
action in a time-bound world, that he commits suicide. But
before completing his deathward movement, Quentin meticulously
arranges his effects in perfect — and meaningless — order. Jason,
too, furiously pursues a selfish order which will allow all bedlam
to enter the Compson world. The futility of secular-materialistic
values as an ordering of the Compson experience is revealed when
the fluctuations of the stock market (the news of which never
reaches him in time) and the flight of Miss Quentin mock his
quest. At the end Benjy is, of course, unaware of the futility of
his more primitive kind of order in the face of existential nothingness; but the chaos he experiences and responds to with moanings
and howlings, and the false order that ironically soothes him,
dramatically frame the entire novel in the same way that Mr.
Compson's sophisticated commentary frames the Quentin section.
It is therefore Mr. Compson, and not Dilsey, whose values finally
prevail. Time is demonstrated to be indeed the *reducto absurdum*
of all human experience.

R. W. Flint said a decade ago that "Faulkner's fiction, made
up as it is of a great many interrelated styles and techniques,
deserves to be called thoroughly composed, *durchkomponiert*, as
the Germans say of music, not only in what it presents but in
what it suggests."[11] Nowhere is the *Durchkomponierung* more
brilliantly manifested than in *The Sound and the Fury*.

---

[11]"Faulkner as Elegist," *Hudson Review*, VII (Summer, 1954), 257.

Michel Gresset

Psychological Aspects of Evil in *The Sound and the Fury*

Like *As I Lay Dying*, but in a much less linear, more elaborate and complex fashion, *The Sound and the Fury* can be described as a novel about an ordeal. This ordeal reveals itself simultaneously upon three levels. The first is individual: the three protagonists who successively hold the center of the stage undergo it of course; but also the character who has been Faulkner's key to the novel, Caddy, and all the others: father and mother and uncle and granddaughter and Luster and Dilsey, like the characters in *As I Lay Dying*, are all involved in one great trial, and the tangled plot of the book follows the consequences, both psychological and moral, of their testing. However, the sum of these individual "agons" is not simply algebraic: it is human, that is to say, living and complex; it constitutes a common ordeal, that of the Compson family and of their Negro servants, and therefore acquires a social and historical value. Lastly, on a third and deeper level, there is in *The Sound and the Fury* that dimension which is characteristic of the symbolistic novel, where the

Revised from *The Mississippi Quarterly*, XIX (Summer 1966). Reprinted by permission of *The Mississippi Quarterly* and the author.

shadows of the poor players fretting their hour in life are cast upon a wider, more metaphysical scale of reference.

The Double Test

What is the nature of this ordeal? From the very beginning, Faulkner's characters are subjected to a double test. On the one hand, they are up against what Faulkner recurrently called "environment"; the reader is supposed to judge them by the yardstick of their ability to integrate themselves in the community and in reality at large. Thus, each of the great Faulknerian heroes embodies, sometimes victoriously but more often pathetically (as Quentin says, "tragedy is secondhand"), the romantic conflict, Solitude versus Society. Their failure shows their inability to resolve this fundamental hiatus between the individual human being and the world.

On the other hand, and on a deeper, even more secret level, the characters undergo the test of their own identities. This is a quest, neither mystical nor cultural nor imposed upon them by exterior, worldly standards, but born out of their very being, through one of those interior necessities that are so characteristic of Faulkner's sense of the human predicament: one of those "compulsions" that account for the opaque, even blind behavior of characters like Quentin or Darl.

I do not feel that it is an oversimplification thus to reduce both the situation and the movement of *The Sound and the Fury* to this double test of identity (i.e., the discovery of harmony with one's own self, and with the world), for it is precisely the organic center from which stem and to which converge all the psychological and even psychic complications which make the novel such a dense, compact and entangled whole, any more than it is a simplification to reduce a ball of string to one thread.

Caddy

It is only natural, in order to unravel the threads of the plot from this point of view, to take up first the character of whom her creator said again and again that it had been his Ariadne's clue: Caddy, woman and essence of woman, a being with whom Faulkner felt in such a close relationship that she could only be described through an aura of epithets, associations, shiftings of registers and symbols: a presence above all, since she is more action than words, more intuition than reasoning, and is not allowed a section like her brothers; but a honeysuckle-intoxicating, full-bodied, triumphant presence. There is no break in her existence, once it is established primarily on the level of sensuality, except for her real, sincere tenderness for Benjy and Quentin: this she does not allow to grow into a fixation, as she easily fills the possible affective gap by transference and natural compensation. She is at once submitted (and wholly submissive) to the eternal laws of femininity, and draws from it her superlative, magnificent physical aura. It does not take her long to solve the only problem with which she is confronted: that of "environment." Within the social unit of the family, integration soon (even precociously) proves impossible: therefore, with no harm done to her conscience nor any obstacle set to her consciousness, she will exclude herself from it, like a foreign body expelled. But her flights, soon followed by her departure, start a disorder within the family not commensurate with the consciousness she had of its consequence. And her relative lack of awareness entails a proportionate lack of responsibility.

The whole family is involved in her failure to grow "normally" from it, and Quentin, unlike Hemingway's character in *A Farewell to Arms*, will not be left "stronger at the broken place." Moreover, according to the ironical laws of Faulkner's tragic time, heredity will weigh upon her own daughter when she is confronted with the same choice: that is, open conflict, or harmony with the family. And Miss Quentin will be even more precocious than her mother.

Thus it can be seen how, in Faulkner's world, nobody can ever say "back to normalcy." Although apparently unconcerned with moral problems as such (a careful parallel with Hawthorne's Pearl might prove of interest), the unsophisticated (in nature) Caddy works evil within the family because she objectively starts a process that will eventually prevent all members from living together on good terms ever again. In other words, there is no "good savage" solution in Faulkner's world. Wild nature, as will be seen with Eula in *The Hamlet*, is no more tolerable from the community's point of view than are oversophistication, psychological complexities and/or moral niceties.

Just as there is about Faulkner's Southern land "a kind of still and violent fecundity" that is both tantalizing and agonizing, the blunt intrusion of nature, of instinct, and especially of sex in the unsteady balance of the family order proves to be no better alternative than the Hamlet-like waverings of Quentin's consciousness. At the beginning, this balance was already precarious; but having lived through two extreme spiritual experiences — one could sum them up under the headings Eros (Caddy) and Thanatos (Quentin) — the family is left shattered beyond repair.

Caddy's failure on the family level is due to such a quality of identity as inevitably tears to pieces the frame that has formed her. She is responsible after all, but only with due respect to that excess of nature with which, as a Faulknerian woman, she is endowed, and which drives her away from the community. Her portrait is a magnificent artistic projection of that quality in woman which always fascinated Faulkner: the tremendous, dumb, secret, brooding, irreducible urge of instinct. Caddy was his favorite child in more than one sense; in his gallery of characters, she is the first achievement of his vision of Eve before the Fall.

Benjy

The idiot of course remains throughout below these problems but he is not left outside the test altogether. For if he is incapable of grasping, as concepts, the two conflicting realities — the ego and the community — whose clash expels his sister and brother, his mind is constantly penetrated by blundering inchoate intuitions of their relationship. The fact of being alive in the world is not problematic for him, for he is on a level with the world (which is ironical enough; but of course there is no "good idiot" solution suggested by Faulkner either): thus the life of his affections (he has one, especially in his relation with his sister — who, apart from Jason, would not fall in love with her?) establishes itself on the level of sensations, immediately translated into tears or well-being, without ever going beyond. Instead of being, like Quentin, the place where good (integration with the real, and realization of identity) and evil (the incapacity to achieve both simultaneously, without letting time, the irremediable, intervene) are at war, he is only the victim of the conflict. A cross for his family, he himself only carries one insofar as, through affective backlashes, he shares in his family's reactions to the common test: Caddy's flight, Quentin's and his father's deaths, Jason's fury. Aesthetically unworthy of a tragic destiny, he can only have that of a living "reducto absurdum of all human experience": he is merely pathetic. A human being for all that in

him is subhuman (his remaining outside awareness, for instance),
he does not escape the common curse: man's propensity to evil.
He will try to rape the passing girls and set the house on fire.
But the very fact that he does not reach awareness leaves him
outside evil; irresponsible, without any consciousness of liberty
and therefore without liberty, he cannot possibly be punished;
his crimes have no existence beyond fact, mere objective fact.
His castration therefore is no punishment: it affects no more than
his body. He and Darl embody two extreme positions, both tan-
gential to evil. As human beings, they are steeped in evil but do
not partake of it.

Quentin

With Quentin the test becomes crucial, in the literal sense.
In him the evil of consciousness waylaid, baffled, disengaged from
reality, is most tragically incarnated. From the start, he owns
more conventional assets than his sister or either of his brothers:
the sale of a meadow pays for his studies at Harvard where,
ironically, his experience of the world amounts to new traumas
that protract and exasperate his idea of an initial fault, his so-
called incest with his sister; this, growing into a destructive obsession, gradually takes on the dreadful aspect of original sin.

All of Quentin's self-knowledge organizes itself around the
image, or the concept, of his sister, of this triumphant feminine
entity which challenges his own, while she irresistibly attracts
and shocks or even outrages him. Thus Quentin, in the crucial
time of adolescence, lets his consciousness be invaded and blocked
by her; no wonder then, that he misses the first test altogether
and remains outside the promised land of identity. Some time
before his suicide, he is found repeating those obsessive phrases
"I was not. I am. I was. I am not." These indeed constitute a
very lucid outline of his own psychological story. Before his
imagined "fall" with Caddy, he was Quentin Compson, a boy,
with prospects of living up to his ancestors' standard. His trau-
matic involvement with Caddy leaves him on the edge of identity,
and he gradually realizes that, with his ego falling beneath the
sheer psychic and moral weight of this experience, life would
become intolerable: why not, then, abolish the whole unbearable
tangle of trauma, fault, and elemental, feminine nature in a
death by water — thus surrendering himself to the very opacity
that his consciousness cannot live with, let alone outlive?

As could be expected with a young man so sensitively involved, his failure in the test of identity entails the same in that of integration. He does not belong in Harvard. His vision of himself in the world tends to become a mere accumulation of refusals until one solution imposes itself upon his mind: that of failure carried, like a cross, to its ultimate consequences: suicide.

Obviously, the process is not as simple as this; the faltering of a knowledge striving after articulation is not without an intricate connection with the failure of communication with his sister which, he so eagerly hoped, might be total (and of course, as a puritan, he chooses not to resolve the fundamental ambiguity of the means to realize this end). As she retreats, repudiating his possessiveness, submitting to the natural call for otherness, for anything else but the narrow, exacting "Compson honor" which is both her brother's obsession and alibi, he too retreats now, no longer from the honor of his family but from reality and finally from life: he carries "the symbol of his frustration into eternity."

Quentin's monologue, a masterpiece of insight and sympathy, displays a mind shut in its own self-constituted vicious circle, and moving inexorably toward the fulfillment of its death-wish.

Jason

Jason undergoes the test simply and effectively; he finds no difficulty whatever in quickly establishing both his identity and his integration: money is the common denominator. In fact he finds them at the lowest possible level: meanness is his main psychological trait. It would remain such, however, were it not repeatedly provoked by his brother, by his sister, and by her daughter: then his meanness takes on a diabolical quality that turns him into an almost archetypal villain. There is irony in the fact that while he has completely renounced the spiritual values of the Compsons, he is the one to provide for their material needs. But there is even more irony when he is ruined by the most tainted, the most "identical" upshoot of the family: the young and sexually precocious Quentin who is Caddy's daughter.

These ironical strokes are not gratuitous. They are the signs of a profoundly organic — neither scientific, nor aesthetic — vision of History (represented by the story of the Compsons) as evincing a twofold movement: linear, of decadence, and cyclic, of fatality. In *The Sound and the Fury* the two combine in a highly effective way, as can be seen clearly in the study of the relationship between children and parents.

The Father

The latter offer a very poor example of harmony indeed, unless it be the entirely negative harmony of incapacity and failure. The uncle is a mere parasite; Benjy, who is a nuisance to the community at large, had first received his uncle's name. The father is a failure on any other level than those of words and alcohol; he is the perfect spokesman for the famous Faulknerian rhetoric, which fills with verbal arabesques the emptiness which is at the core of the being, just as the baroque aesthetics filled the dreaded void with curves. Himself incapable of living in any other present but the golden and dusty time of his ancestors, he hands over to Quentin, with the watch, his superb but vain piece of advice: "I give you the mausoleum of all hope and desire."

His death leaves no real gap in the family: his absence is only felt as that of a decorative link in the chain of the Compson memory (which probably explains the surreptitious presence of Caddy at his burial). As a father, he is of course an utter failure.

The Mother

Even worse is the model offered by the mother. She is completely alienated from her part, from her place in and of the family. Instead of taking on her responsibilities, she lets Dilsey, Luster, or Jason shoulder them. Morever, what makes her odious is her constant desire to fill with words the void, the absence, the failure that she is and that she is fully aware of being. Her recurrent, wailing auto-criticism makes her one of the rare thoroughly unlikable feminine characters in Faulkner's work: a worthy mother of Jason the villain. Her only merit — and her useful function — is to illuminate the key problem in the common ordeal: that of identity, which, as a woman, she approaches through heredity and names: Jason can cope with reality: therefore he is not a Compson but a Bascomb. And of course she is right in a way: though not a rational explanation, this serves as a clue to our understanding of the book. And what she wishes for her granddaughter is terrible, indeed, but very significant: that she may have neither a father nor a name.

The Name

On a purely verbal level, the mother wishes for her grand-children what her own children seek with their muscles and even with their lives: an identity. She does not contradict herself when she says "I knew the minute they named her Quentin this would happen." This of course is only an onlooker's comment; but she does put her finger upon what she calls the "curse," the impingement of time on the consciousness, from which arises the problem of identity. (Jason shows the extent to which he shares his mother's viewpoint when he calls Caddy "a woman that cant name the father of her own child.") She hints at the terrible legacy of splendor and shame (and time has diminished the former while increasing the latter) bequeathed to contemporaries by their ancestors in those clans where evil spread and even worsens the pattern set by the mother who cannot even name her child's father.

It is clearer now how this poem of evil is composed. Structurally, the book seems to leave no other way of triumphing over circumstances but idiocy, suicide, mammonism, and prostitution.

The Negroes

Admirably coherent as it is, Faulkner's profound and searching analysis of the working of evil within and between the consciousness of the Compsons is further reinforced by the counterpoint supplied by the Negroes. Here we enter a world that seems to have nothing in common with the other, and whose only link with it is the stubborn adhesion of their servants to a family even until its complete disintegration.

For Roskus, who dies in harness; for Frony; for T. P.; for Luster, so precociously manly and yet so meanly childish; and above all for Dilsey, who is both a superb major creation and the living embodiment of so many (though not all) of the virtues extolled by Faulkner at Stockholm, there is no problem that is not solved daily, in and by the very flow of life. The Negroes' time is horizontal, while the Compsons' is vertical with a downward and whirling movement. Instead of being led to "end them" by vainly trying to oppose their troubles with their puny weapons, like the whites, the Negroes "suffer the slings and arrows of outrageous fortune." In calmness and dignity (two of the rare virtues that Faulkner and Hemingway both admire), they cope with a world in which the Compsons are failures. This success is obvious in Dilsey, and even in Luster, but it is not simple: for on the one hand, through one of those ironies that Faulkner has so well shown to lie in the Southern tragedy, the Negroes are at least partially robbed of their sense of identity because so much depends on age-old customs, going back to slavery (e.g. Jason's attitude, who constantly sets the Negroes "in their place"); on the other they do not have this legacy of glory and fault weighing so heavily upon them. Their community is not even looked upon by the whites as a possible model for salvation.

By comparison with the harsh, jarring, pessimistic picture of evil in the consciousness of the white people, one may find this vision of a stereotyped "good" Negro who is neither a drinker nor a thief nor a fornicator rather idealized. There is, no doubt, a note of personal gratitude and affection in Dilsey's portrait, as thirteen years later, Faulkner was to show in the dedication of *Go Down Moses*:

> "To Mammy Caroline Barr, Mississippi (1840-1940). Who was born in slavery and who gave to my family a fidelity without stint or calculation of recompense and to my childhood an immeasurable devotion and love."

But it is clear, and will certainly be made clearer by further studies, how much the work owes to the biography — not so much to factual, or anecdotal, biography as to a kind of affective and spiritual autobiography. This, far from reducing Faulkner's stature, will on the contrary emphasize and enhance his tremendous power as a creator, quite unique in twentieth century American literature.

Method

The main point of this essay has been to suggest a modest reading of Faulkner's work that, contrary to all ambitious "exterior" approaches (Christian, existentialist, Marxist, psychoanalytic, etc.), focuses primarily not on the ideas behind the writing, but on what actually takes place in the course of the story: both on the structure and on the texture of the work.

This is particularly important as regards the problem of evil. Any critic who approaches Faulkner's work with a preconceived idea of what he will find there is bound to harvest what *he*, not

Faulkner, has sown. In so complex and elaborate work of art as *The Sound and the Fury* especially, it seems better — more responsible and also more modest — to begin with as careful a consideration as possible of the *working* of evil within the consciousness. After all, it may be hard to decide whether Faulkner was above all a metaphysician or a novelist, besides being, as we all know from his repeating it so often, a story teller; but he certainly was more than slightly interested in psychology: first because this was the "camino real" to his people's souls; second because the deeper he probed into them, the more exciting the challenge became to his technique as a craftsman.

Moreover, his work is grounded on solid realities like family and community, not on ideas, and even less or theories, be they sociological or psychoanalytical. He never, even in *A Fable*, had a thesis as his purpose. He just stole from every possible source, confessed to it unabashedly, and of course was right from beginning to end. If he had needed a sponsor, Balzac was there, and Dickens too. His greatest source of plunder was the South.

What is a family, or a community, or even a population, but a gathering of individuals, therefore of consciousnesses, brought and held together by all sorts of links? Faulkner was not a philosopher; evil, to him, was not an abstraction, but a part of reality, immanent, pervasive, tangible, and permanent, like time. Both the structure and the style of *The Sound and the Fury* show (1) evil to be woven into the working of the consciousness as well as brooding and lurking over and around it, like Southern storms, and (2) irony to lie in the cyclic recurrence of the same impact of time upon the consciousness. The study of Evil inevitably leads one to that of Time and its effect upon the human "psyche," with Irony as the great lesson to be drawn. Irony is the sign both of God's sneering indifference (as in Thomas Hardy) and of Man's utter impotence (as in more contemporary novelists like Samuel Beckett).

That Faulkner used the Bible — and he did, of course: just as he *used* the South; everything in him was devoted to his literary creation — is no reason why one could not read the old concepts of damnation and redemption in the characters' minds, with the old key of psychology. Identity, integration: the other critical step consists in seeing what happens to the characters or rather how they come out: do they survive? do they perish? There are no such things as "happy endings" in Faulkner's fiction. The way he wanted his stories to end is a main clue to our understanding of his general intention.

Well, there is not much hope left for the family at the end of this book. In spite of Dilsey and the superb passage about the great Negro Easter Sunday (one of the finest musical pieces in modern literature), *The Sound and the Fury* ends with Benjy's voice roaring and roaring before hushing as everything takes "its ordered place" again; but only through an idiot's sense of order can it be said that Good and Evil resume their position; and he is below the level of choice. For the family, "what is done cannot be undone," and evil has passed repair. There is no hope left because the consciousnesses, apart from Jason's or the villain's, have given way. In Faulkner's work the order of the world is conservative; it rests on the individual and on the family and on the community, in a progressive opening up upon the cosmos. In this, Faulkner is the last link in the great chain of Anglo-American symbolistic writers: in France, the only equivalent is to be found in poetry.

Besides being, since Melville's *Moby-Dick*, one of the few truly Shakespearian books of the past century, *The Sound and the Fury* is both Faulkner's *Waste Land* and his *Saison en Enfer*.

Michael Millgate

The Problem of Point of View

Nothing in Faulkner's career is more remarkable than the sheer bulk of his achievement and the extraordinary range of his experimentation, the variety of narrative techniques adopted in successive volumes. Even his earliest novels, *Soldiers' Pay* and *Mosquitoes*, incorporated distinctive experimental elements, and by the time he wrote his fourth novel, *The Sound and the Fury*, he was no longer tinkering with the problems of fictional form but undertaking radical new departures. Three of the four sections of *The Sound and the Fury* take the form of interior monologues; *As I Lay Dying*, his next book is entirely made up of a series of interior monologues radiating from the central "story" like the spokes of a wheel. In other books of the 1930's and early 1940's the experiments were of many different kinds: chiefly stylistic in *Pylon*, chiefly structural in *The Wild Palms*, both stylistic and structural in *Absalom, Absalom!*, *The Hamlet*, and *Go Down, Moses*.

From Marston LaFrance, ed. *Patterns of Commitment in American Literature* (Toronto: University of Toronto Press, 1967). Reprinted by permission of University of Toronto Press and the author.

After the war, and particularly in his last three novels, *The Town*, *The Mansion*, and *The Reivers*, Faulkner tended more and more to abandon this experimental exuberance and confine himself to fictional techniques which were less obviously innovatory. It is possible, of course, that the relatively conventional character of the late fiction represents simply a falling-off in energy, but that this may not be the whole answer is suggested by the presence among Faulkner's later work of *Requiem for a Nun*, a kind of play-within-a-novel (or, if you prefer it, a play in which the opening stage direction of each act has the length and indeed the structure of a short story), and also of *A Fable*, an intricately constructed narrative which is, perhaps, not so much a novel as what its title announces it to be — a fable, a moral exemplum, eloquent of general truths. Apparently Faulkner neither rejected experimentation as such nor lost the energy with which to conduct experiments when they seemed to be called for. Is it possible then — and it is to this question that I want to address myself in this paper — that Faulkner may have felt in writing the more conventional of his final novels that he had in fact found not a retreat or a respite from, but actually an answer to, those very problems which had earlier led him into more evidently adventurous paths?

These problems all involved in some degree the question of point of view, an area of technique which is not only of fundamental importance to all novelists but which has characteristically been a major preoccupation of modern novelists, and particularly of Conrad and Joyce, two of the most powerful and most immediate influences on Faulkner himself. The problem of point of view embraces, after all, some of the most crucial questions of literary technique: from whose angle and in whose voice is the story told? Where does authority lie in the novel, and whom, as readers, should we trust? Where does the author himself stand, and how do we *know* where he stands? We have to ask such questions, and answer them satisfactorily, before we can speak with any assurance of the moral patterning of a book or even, in some instances, of what it is, in the broadest sense, about.

What is immediately striking is the rarity of the first-person narrator in Faulkner's work. In a writer who is so often claimed as a direct descendant of Mark Twain and the tradition of Southwestern humour, it is a little surprising to find only two books — *The Unvanquished* and *The Reivers* — which are told entirely from the point of view of a single first-person narrator. And even in *The Reivers* the first-person narrator is not the final authority: the whole book is thrust into a frame, set at a distance, by the implications of the two opening words — "Grandfather said" — and of the colon which follows them.[1] The content of the book may be Grandfather's story, but clearly we must suppose that story to have been set down not by Grandfather himself but by one of his audience, presumably a grandson, and the distinction is crucial to a proper apprehension of the tone of the whole book. Henry James, of course, had a horror of "the terrible *fluidity* of self-revelation," and Faulkner, with his own highly developed sense of form, may conceivably have seen similar dangers in this particular technique. But obviously there is more to it than that, and even as one notes the relative absence of direct first-person narrative in Faulkner's work, one is haunted by the sense that the spoken voice is one of the dominant elements in almost all of his books. What closer inspection reveals is that many of his novels have not a single point of view at all but a multiplicity of points of view and, further, that Faulkner's preference is, in many cases, for a multiplicity of types of point of view — first person, third person, stream of consciousness, centre of consciousness, and so on. Perhaps it would be useful, as a way of clarifying this question, to look in a little more detail at one particular book, *The Sound and the Fury*, generally thought of as the most "difficult" and technically adventurous of Faulkner's works.

A reader who comes unprepared to the opening section of the novel may well be initially at a loss to know into what kind of a fictional world he has strayed:

> Through the fence, between the curling flower spaces, I could see them hitting. They were coming toward where the flag was and I went along the fence. Luster was hunting in the grass by the flower tree. They took the flag out, and they were hitting. Then they put the flag back and they went to the table, and he hit and the other hit. Then they went on, and I went along the fence. Luster came away from the flower tree and we went along the fence and they stopped and we stopped and I looked through the fence while Luster was hunting in the grass.
>
> "Here, caddie." He hit. They went away across the pasture. I held to the fence and watched them going away. [p. 1]

The reader may well wonder who it is speaking in this curiously formal, elaborately simple way. It may take some time for him

---

[1] Faulkner, *The Reivers* (New York: Random House, 1962), p. 3.

to realize that what he is hearing is not properly a speaking voice at all; that he is, in fact, inside the mind of Benjy Compson, a thirty-three-year-old idiot. Benjy cannot talk; nor is he capable, in even the simplest of ways, of distinguishing the relation of cause and effect; and what Faulkner does in this whole section of the novel is establish a convention of pure objectivity. Benjy observes the world around him, but he is incapable of imposing any pattern on that observation, and Faulkner employs him as a kind of camera-eye, recording whatever passes before him.

In that opening paragraph, Benjy is in the garden of the Compson house, looking through the fence and the honeysuckle ("the curling flower spaces") at men playing golf ("hitting") on the adjoining course. When one of the golfers calls out "Here, caddie," Benjy howls in anguish ("I held to the fence," he says), and it is not till some time later that we realize he is giving voice to that vague sense of loss he feels at the absence of his sister Caddy, the one member of the family on whom he had depended for comfort. It is only later, too, that we discover that the golf course was formerly Benjy's pasture, one of the few things in the world to which he felt an attachment, and that the land has been sold to pay for a Harvard education for Benjy's brother, Quentin. Later still, we discover that Caddy has left home in disgrace, that Quentin has committed suicide at the end of his first year at Harvard, that Jason, the youngest of the Compson children and the only one left at home with Benjy, is a mean and rapacious small business man. The Compson family had once been a relatively distinguished one in the society of Mississippi, but it is now in the process of rapid disintegration, hastened rather than delayed by the cynicism of a dipsomaniac father, now dead, and the utter selfishness of a neurotic mother, still alive and still complaining.

The reader discovers these things as he gets further and further into the book, as he responds to that experience of progressive discovery and imaginative re-creation to which Faulkner's technique invites and, indeed, compels him. Benjy is narrator of the first section, Quentin of the second, Jason of the third, while the fourth section is told by the familiar method of third-person narration, in which the author puts himself in a position of omniscience. Each of the first three sections is a *tour de force* in its own way: in Benjy's section, as we have seen, there is that brilliantly achieved convention of objectivity and an absolute freedom of movement backwards and forwards in time — the creation of what Faulkner once described in a letter as "that unbroken-surfaced confusion of an idiot which is outwardly a dynamic and logical coherence."[2] Quentin's section is the interior monologue not of an idiot but of a highly sensitive and extremely tortured mind, and we follow, in a variation of the Joycean stream-of-consciousness method, the various experiences, ideas, images, memories which crowd upon his over-active mind during the last day of his life. Jason's section is an extremely successful capturing of a particular personality in terms of a particular tone of voice: "Like I say if all the businesses in a town are run like country businesses, you're going to have a country town" (p. 310). When Jason talks like that, the man and his attitudes come frighteningly alive for us; one might add, too, that although this section, like its two predecessors, is generally spoken of as an interior monologue, the voice evoked is specifically a speaking voice, and it is easy to imagine Jason's words as being spoken out loud. This is much less true of Benjy's and Quentin's sections, and it is perhaps a sign that in this third section we are already moving outwards from the extreme internalization of the first two sections to the overtly social world of the fourth section, in which Faulkner writes as the omniscient author and gives us, for the first time, a physical description of the various members of the Compson family and of the Compson estate, and shows us much more clearly than before the ways in which the Compsons and their Negro retainers relate to the large society of Jefferson, Mississippi.

But why — it might be asked, and with some passion — why do it this way at all? Faulkner once said that in *The Sound and the Fury* he had told the same story four times,[3] but that will hardly do as a complete explanation: the four sections may illustrate the same fundamental situation, that of the Compson family in its decay, but there is not in fact a great deal of narrative overlapping from one section to another. Indeed, the powerfully evoked individuality of the three first-person narrators, each locked in his own kind of unreality and remoteness, tends to result in a certain lack of over-all cohesion in the novel, and although one of Faulkner's chief purposes seems to have been the creation of

---

[2]Michael Millgate, *The Achievement of William Faulkner* (New York: Random House, 1966), p. 94.
[3]James B. Meriwether and Michael Millgate, eds. *Lion in the Garden: Interviews with William Faulkner, 1926-1962* (New York: Random House, 1968), p. 147.

Caddy, the Compson daughter, in terms of the viewpoints of her
three brothers, there is a sense in which she remains vague and
elusive of definition. It would be extremely interesting to know
whether Faulkner had originally intended to write the fourth
section in the third person, or whether his decision to do so
was in some degree the result of a sense that the book was in
danger of falling apart and needed a kind of authorial hoop to
hold it together. It is not hard, in fact, to see ample justification
for Faulkner's decision to write the closing section as he did —
it was the most appropriate way of handling a considerable body
of narrative material and it gave the reader release from the
claustrophobic intensity of the previous sections. But although
The Sound and the Fury was the book of which Faulkner spoke
with most affection in later years, he seems at the same time
to have thought of it as at least a partial failure,[4] and one of the
sources of his dissatisfaction may have been an awareness that,
given the basic technique of the novel, there were other Compson
voices that should perhaps have been allowed to make themselves
heard: Caddy's, her daughter's, Mr. Compson's, Mrs. Compson's,
Dilsey's.

In *As I Lay Dying,* of course, that is precisely what Faulkner
did: everyone is given a voice — not only every member of the
Bundren family, but also several neighbours and various other
people whom the Bundrens encounter on their way to Jefferson.
Unity can be said to have been achieved here simply by virtue
of the comprehensiveness of the points of view, but it is more
specifically achieved by the way in which each of the narrative
fragments makes its own contribution to the central "story" —
the anecdote of the journey itself. It is a brilliant *tour de force*,
but one which could only be achieved, perhaps, with basic material
of this limited and essentially anecdotal kind. It is hard to see
how the four sections of *The Sound and the Fury* could have
been very much shorter than they are, and it seems likely that
if Faulkner had attempted to deal in the *As I Lay Dying* manner
with material on the scale of *The Sound and the Fury* he would
have found himself with a book unmanageable in terms simply
of size alone.

There may well have been other reasons, however, why Faulkner
did not repeat the kind of experiments in the use of the first-
person narrator which he had undertaken in *The Sound and the*

[4]*Ibid.*

Fury and *As I Lay Dying*. He may have recognized a more fundamental limitation in exclusive reliance on first-person narration, however generously proliferated. Use of the first-person point of view can give vitality and immediacy; it allows the novelist both to tell the story, to recount simple narrative events, and, at the same time, to reveal the character of the narrator himself — in terms of the way the story is told, the order in which events are recounted, what is emphasized and dwelt upon, and, certainly not least, the kind of language that is used. But how are we to judge the reliability of what the narrator tells us? How, specifically, does the author dissociate himself from an untrustworthy first-person narrator? Clearly, a skillful author can make a narrator like Jason Compson betray his unreliability by everything he says; an alternative method of ironic self-revelation is to allow the narrative itself to involve patterns of events — or simply passages of dialogue — which irresistibly call in question the narrator's interpretation of them. By such methods the author can invoke in the novel, in however shadowy a form, an ideal standard of value against which the narrator's aberrations can be assessed. The method has its limitations, however. The measurement of human behaviour against abstract standards, whether aesthetic or moral, is not necessarily a particularly sensitive process, and the attempt to enforce judgment of a first-person narrator in terms of standards both abstract and only tenuously implicit may well become oversimplified and much too absolute.

Because Faulkner preferred to judge people in terms not of abstractions but of responses to actual human situations, his view of the world, of human behaviour, and of human values was rather more complex than this, and in writing *Light in August*, his next major novel after *As I Lay Dying*, he attempted to give expression to that complexity. In technical terms this involved considerable modification of his use of first-person narration, which now took a subsidiary rôle instead of the dominant one it had been given in previous books. *Light in August*, indeed, is the novel in which Faulkner first tried to incorporate within a relatively conventional framework the kind of narrative effects he had sought, and in large measure obtained, in *The Sound and the Fury* and *As I Lay Dying* — but perhaps at the cost of drawing disproportionate attention to the techniques themselves. In *Light in August* Faulkner still avoids simple chronological continuity and still deals, as he was to do throughout his career, in large blocks of material so disposed as to achieve maximum effects of

ironic juxtaposition or to bring to bear the fullest possible weight
of historical, social, and emotional complexity upon a particular
moment in time. The long flashback telling the story of Joe
Christmas, the man who does not know whether he is Negro or
white, is thus poised, in point of time, on the moment just before
the final and fatal confrontation between Joe himself and Joanna
Burden, the aging white woman who has become his mistress.
The novel contains several substantial passages of first-person
narrative — by Miss Burden, by Gavin Stevens, by the mad Doc
Hines and his wife, by the anonymous furniture dealer in the
final chapter, and by a voice identified simply as "they" — the
ordinary people of the town of Jefferson and its surrounding
countryside. But while these passages often continue uninterrupted
at some length, and thus retain a degree of independent identity,
they are all incorporated into an over-all narrative framework.

The most remarkable of these passages, structurally speaking,
is the final account by the furniture dealer of his encounter with
Lena Grove and the doggedly faithful Byron Bunch. The account
is essentially a monologue, an extended passage of first-person
narration, but it is interrupted from time to time by comments
from the man's wife, and we become quickly aware that the
telling of this mildly racy story is considerably affected by the
presence of this particular audience and by the fact that the two
of them are together in bed. At one level, of course, this is very
much in the tradition of American anecdotal humour — the humor-
ous story, according to Mark Twain, is essentially American and
its point consists primarily in the way it is told — but as one
looks at the other examples of first-person narrative in *Light in
August* it becomes clear that each of them is addressed to a
specific audience and that each of them is affected, to a greater
or lesser degree, by the speaker's awareness of that audience (Doc
Hines, perhaps, is oblivious of his particular audience, but it
might well be argued that this was precisely an aspect of his
madness). Our own total experience as we read these passages
includes — or should include, if we are reading sufficiently closely
— simultaneous awareness of the speaker and of his audience,
and of the interaction of the two.

Faulkner's great innovation in *Absalom, Absalom!*, published
four years after *Light in August*, was to make this awareness
into an organizing principle. He realized that first-person narrative, with all its advantages of immediacy and character revelation, need not be treated in isolation — as separate sections of

uninterrupted solo performance — but could be handled in terms of extended dialogue. From this point on, it might almost be said, Faulkner's characteristic way of handling narrative was to present it as a recital to an audience, a monologue with interruptions. The great advantage of interrupted monologue, as Faulkner discovered, was that it permitted interior and exterior views of a character to be much more closely juxtaposed and virtually, indeed, to coexist. Because an audience is present, the characters are quite naturally driven to deal not simply with events but with motivation, to reveal the bases of reason, prejudice, or emotion on which they have acted — or on which they believe themselves to have acted. The listeners, for their part, may abandon silence to protest, argue, cross-examine, or engage in Socratic dialogue — as Gavin Stevens so frequently does, for instance, in the play sections of *Requiem for a Nun*.

In *Absalom, Absalom!* itself, the whole complex structure is built up almost entirely from the interlocking of a succession of interrupted monologues, and Faulkner once described Shreve McCannon, the arch-interrupter, as "the commentator that held the thing to something of reality," adding: "If Quentin had been let alone to tell it, it would have become completely unreal. It had to have a solvent to keep it real, keep it believable, creditable, otherwise it would have vanished into smoke and fury."[5] There is perhaps a hint here of the kind of function performed by the interlocutors in other Faulkner novels: the disgusted interjections of the short convict as the tall convict tells his tale in the "Old Man" section of *The Wild Palms* represent, in one respect, just such an intrusion of the voice of common sense. To put it another way, they are in some degree the kind of interjections which we as readers should be making, and it is almost as though Faulkner had provided the reader with a second self within the very world of the novel.

By methods such as these, the first-person narrator can be judged not simply against standards implicit in his own narrative, but in terms of concurrent commentary from a specific audience. Ironic effects proceed now not so much from verbal jugglery within the monologue itself as from the juxtaposition of monologue and context, the relation between what is said and the situation in which it is said: the tall convict's tale of freedom

---

[5]Frederick L. Gwynn and Joseph L. Blotner, eds., *Faulkner in the University: Class Conferences at the University of Virginia, 1957-1958* (Charlottesville: University of Virginia Press, 1959), p. 75.

unappreciated is being related, after all, to an audience of con-
victs still hopelessly immured. It is in *The Wild Palms*, of course,
that Faulkner made the most obviously challenging of his experiments in large-scale ironic juxtaposition, since it seems clear that
the story of the tall convict, embarrassed by a freedom he did not
seek or desire, was designed by Faulkner as a deliberate counterpoint to the story of Charlotte Rittenmeyer and Harry Wilbourne,
who suffered every kind of agony in their search for a freedom
they could never attain.[6] Such a juxtaposition relates directly
to the question of point of view, for our evaluation of the meaning
of either story must be profoundly affected by our having been
forced to a parallel reading of its companion piece: the meaning
of the novel as a whole is precisely the product of our reaction
to this experience, our response to the coexistence, the chapter
by chapter alternation, of two stories which may look and be
quite separate as simple narrative but which Faulkner insists
are related in significant ways.

   The Wild Palms was published in 1939; *The Hamlet*, a novel of
great beauty and remarkable stylistic virtuosity, appeared in 1940;
and in 1942 came *Go Down, Moses*, perhaps the most widely and
persistently misunderstood of all Faulkner's works. In *Go Down,
Moses*, I suggest, Faulkner is demanding still more of us than he
did in *The Wild Palms*, though few critics seem even to have
realized that he is demanding anything at all. Misunderstanding
of the book began with its first editor, who took it upon himself
to call the volume *Go Down, Moses and other Stories;* that "and
other Stories" was a quite unauthorized addition which Faulkner
later had cancelled but which has bedeviled discussion of the book
ever since.[7] The so-called stories which make up *Go Down, Moses*
were intended by Faulkner to be read as chapters in a novel;[8]
each of them makes a quite distinct statement about white-Negro
relations or about the destruction of the wilderness, or about
both, and our reading of the book as a whole must depend upon
our awareness of the interaction of all these separate statements
one with another. We tend to look for neater, more clearly formulated resolutions in most of the books we read, but Faulkner's
deliberate choice, here as elsewhere, is to offer as resolution the
fact of complexity itself, the frank acknowledgment that there

---

[6] *Lion in the Garden*, p. 132.
[7] For a discussion of this point see *The Achievement of William Faulkner*,
pp. 202-3.
[8] *Faulkner in the University*, pp. 4, 273.

may be situations — such as the white-Negro situation — in which no single standard of right and wrong is universally applicable, and in which men of goodwill can only do what seems to them right and necessary and possible in any given set of circumstances. The fourth section of "The Bear" is the one point in the novel where Faulkner attempts to bring all his material into narrower focus, and he does so precisely by means of that technique of interrupted monologue we have already discussed. The basic monologue here is Ike McCaslin's, but because Ike is delivering it to his cousin Cass, a man who has adopted different solutions to the very problems which so agitate Ike himself, the whole section becomes a kind of debate, a dramatized presentation of what are essentially abstract issues. Faced with the problem of living as moral men in an immoral world — specifically here, the world of the American South — Ike has chosen withdrawal into idealism, Cass involvement in the sometimes sordid world of actuality; Faulkner is not necessarily here saying that either is right or wrong, but rather that Ike's position, however dignified, looks a good deal less admirable when put side by side with the practical workaday achievements of Cass, while Cass's position, though sensible and practical, certainly lacks idealism and perhaps contributes to the perpetuation of social evils.[9]

Go Down, Moses was the logical culmination of directions which Faulkner's work had been taking for several years previously, and there is no reason to think that he was dissatisfied with it. Nevertheless, its particular solution was not to be his final solution; it is characteristic of Faulkner, indeed, that he regarded no solution as final but tried always to avoid repeating himself in any way, to do something fresh in every book. What he attempted several years later in *Requiem for a Nun* was to isolate the interrupted monologue in the form of a play; his relative failure in this book was perhaps not so much a matter of the basic conception but of the highly artificial dialogue in which he chose to embody it. He did not, at any rate, abandon the idea of disengaging the monologue from the traditional kind of novel structure, even though to attempt to do so was in some sense to retrace the steps he had taken in working towards the integrated structure of novels like *Absalom, Absalom!* and *The Hamlet.*

---

[9]For a somewhat similar dramatization of an ideological conflict, see the interview between the Corporal and the old General in *A Fable* (New York: Random House, 1954), pp. 342-56.

When, in the middle 1950's, Faulkner resumed the writing of the Snopes trilogy, of which the first volume, *The Hamlet*, had been published many years before, he worked out another solution to the problem of point of view — a solution less dramatic than many of his earlier experiments but precisely calculated to meet the particular demands of his material and themes. In *The Town*, the second volume of the Snopes trilogy, the narration is divided between three first-person narrators, Gavin Stevens, V. K. Ratliff, and Charles Mallison. Gavin Stevens is the central character, and his sections of narrative give expression to his hopelessly romantic attitudes towards first Eula Varner and then her daughter Linda. Ratliff, a man of very different outlook, operates to some extent as the reader's representative within the novel, and his comments on Stevens' romantic notions, though often brief, are extremely pointed. Charles Mallison, as Stevens' nephew, gives us glimpses of his uncle in domestic situations, but he also speaks specifically as the voice of Jefferson, as a mouthpiece for the local consensus: "So when I say 'we' and 'we thought' what I mean is Jefferson and what Jefferson thought."[10] The novel achieves unity through the continuity of the narrative as it is passed on, relay fashion, from one narrator to another, and through the carefully established sense of Jefferson itself as a place and a society. This unity is also greatly strengthened by the way in which the three narrators, and particularly Ratliff and Charles, seem to engage in a continual conversation. For Ratliff and Charles the conversation is usually about Stevens, and if Stevens, on the other hand, seems often to be talking to himself, that is, perhaps, precisely a sign of his relative isolation from reality.

Although *The Town* is not often thought of as one of Faulkner's major achievements, it perhaps deserves greater recognition as a novel in which Faulkner seems finally to have come to terms with the problem of point of view with which he had wrestled so long. By means of the efficient but quite unobtrusive technique he has here adopted, Faulkner has retained all the normal advantages of first-person narrative; at the same time, he has not sacrificed economy, because he has used only three narrators, each of whom fulfils a major representative rôle, as well as a purely individual one, in the over-all pattern; he has not sacrificed unity, because the successive narrative sections all contribute to a single developing story; he has not sacrificed those advantages of continuing

---

[10]Faulkner, *The Town* (New York: Random House, 1957), p. 3.

commentary which came with the interrupted monologue, because the placing of many of the sections, particularly those in which Ratliff is the narrator, is designed precisely to fulfil such a function; nor has he sacrificed complexity, since our total response, as in *The Wild Palms* or *Go Down, Moses*, depends upon our awareness not only of Gavin Stevens' view of things but also of the very different views of Ratliff and Charles Mallison and the people of Jefferson. Stevens may operate at some distance from what most of us would regard as the world of practical reality, but we are not allowed to view him in such isolation, any more than we are allowed to view him entirely on his own terms. The characters of the novel include Ratliff and Eula Varner as well as Gavin Stevens, and what finally confronts us here, as in all of Faulkner's works, is not man alone, or man judged against an abstract ideal, but man seen in relation to his fellow men and in the context of his society, doing what he can and must within the inescapable limitations of an actual and highly imperfect world — or, in Stevens' case, refusing, grandly but foolishly, to recognize such limitations at all.

Because of his treatment of such "lost" characters as Joe Christmas in *Light in August* and Quentin Compson in both *The Sound and the Fury* and *Absalom, Absalom!*, and because of his recourse in *The Sound and the Fury* and *As I Lay Dying* to the extreme intimacies of stream-of-consciousness technique, Faulkner has often been thought of as a quintessentially "modern" novelist, dealing primarily with the agonies of contemporary man in his desperate search for identity and expression. Unquestionably this element is present in Faulkner's work, and especially in the novels just mentioned. When Faulkner gave his Nobel Prize address, however, these were not the themes on which he dwelt: he spoke rather of "the old verities and truths of the heart, the old universal truths lacking which any story is ephemeral and doomed — love and honor and pity and pride and compassion and sacrifice."[11] If one accepts that the Nobel Prize speech was not an idle rhetorical exercise but a precise expression of what Faulkner believed his work to be about, then clearly one has to see Faulkner's major emphasis as falling not so much on the individual in isolation as on the individual in his relation to other human beings. Faulkner, indeed, seems "traditional," rather than "modern," in his insistence

---

[11]James B. Meriwether, ed., *Essays, Speeches, and Public Letters by William Faulkner* (New York: Random House, 1965), p. 120.

on questions of right conduct, and it might well be argued that the major themes in his work, taken as a whole, are essentially social in character.

Cleanth Brooks has written very persuasively of the importance of responding, in almost every Faulkner novel, to the omnipresent sense of the community, "the powerful though invisible force that quietly exerts itself in so much of Faulkner's work. It is the circumambient atmosphere, the essential ether of Faulkner's fiction."[12] As Brooks goes on to point out, we become aware of the community in a novel like *Light in August* in terms of the minor characters and their reactions to the central characters, and, even more explicitly, in terms of that unidentified voice which speaks for the community as a whole and of the furniture dealer's final picture of Lena Grove and Byron Bunch — a picture which, because of its frankness and humour, serves to place not only the affairs of Lena and Byron but the whole action of the novel in a new perspective. The final section of *The Sound and the Fury* performs a somewhat analogous function, and even in *As I Lay Dying* the passionate voices of the Bundrens in their intensely introspective monologues are counterpointed against a kind of composite voice of the community, made up of the monologues of the various outsiders who become involved in the story. Even in these most aggressively "modern" of his novels, Faulkner found it necessary to give some direct expression to the social reverberations of individual action, and in subsequent works the presence of society, of the community, becomes even more apparent. The very device of the interrupted monologue, the very presence of an audience for most of the passages of first-person narrative, even the book-length narrative of *The Reivers* — the use of such techniques implies almost automatically the existence of a specific social situation.

Master of technique though he was, Faulkner knew that technique is meaningless if it is pursued simply for its own sake, and in book after book he resisted the temptations of the spectacular and worked towards the perfection of technical devices whose very unobtrusiveness would best subserve his over-all objective of presenting the human condition in all its pain, joy, hope, despair, defeat, and triumph. "Art is simpler than people think," Faulkner wrote to Malcolm Cowley in 1945, "because there is so little to

---

[12]*William Faulkner: The Yoknapatawpha Country* (New Haven: Yale University Press, 1963), p. 52.

write about. All the moving things are eternal in man's history and have been written before, and if a man writes hard enough, sincerely enough, humbly enough, and with the unalterable determination never never never to be quite satisfied with it he will repeat them, because art like poverty takes care of its own, shares it bread."[13]

---

[13]*The Achievement of William Faulkner*, p. 252.

Richard Gunter

Style and Language in
The Sound and the Fury

Style in a work of literature may be either personal or functional. When it is merely personal it is nothing more than the
author's presence. That presence may be obtrusive or self-effacing,
pleasing or annoying, but it is peripheral to the work itself. But
when style is functional it becomes a fundamental part of the
work. In the novel, for example, style may function in dialogue
and monologue to create character. Although this use of style is
somewhat neglected by the critics, it is a powerful device. It
deserves the most careful study.

An author can evoke a whole range of distinct characters
merely by having them speak in certain ways. The process is
complex and subtle. It rests upon the reader's knowledge of
people and speech in the real world. In that world the reader will
have met many persons, will have heard them speak, and will

An essay-review of Irena Kaluza, *The Functioning of Sentence Structure in
the Stream-of-Consciousness Technique of William Faulkner's 'The Sound
and the Fury': A Study in Linguistic Stylistics*, Krakow: Nakladem Uni-
wersytetu Jagiellonskiego, 1967. From *The Mississippi Quarterly*, XII (Summer 1969). Reprinted by permission of *The Mississippi Quarterly* and the
author.

have stored away — all unconsciously — many memories of their traits, associated with their ways of speaking. The author can draw upon this bank of memory by having his creature say words, phrases and sentences that strike chords in the reader. Thus the reader is led to reassemble bits and pieces of old impressions into a new constellation, so that in imagination he constructs a new fictional character. It must be stressed that this process may go far beyond verismilitude: it is not merely that the author first depicts characters by other means, then gives them appropriate language to say; it is rather that their speech can itself be the means for depicting them.

For the present purpose it is useful to think of character in two senses. In the first sense character is social identity. Every person in a society is a bundle of the roles and statuses that sociologists like to talk about. Each is a member of certain groups, and the sum of his memberships is his social identity. Thus one may be male, middle-aged, a banker, a husband, a Methodist and the like. Or one may be female, young, single, a stenographer and the like. These are social identities.

The dialect that each person speaks is also a part of his social identity; in fact it is an index to the other features in the bundle. Bankers tend to talk like bankers, laborers like laborers, women like women. Speech is a rich set of clues to who we are, for the dialect structure of the country mirrors its social structure. The skillful novelist — William Faulkner, for instance — makes good use of this fact.

Character in the second sense is much more subtle and much more interesting. It is what remains when social identity is stripped away. It is personality — motive, self, mentality. This side of character can also be revealed through speech in literature, and the possibility of such revelation likewise rests upon the reader's experience with people and their language, and especially upon the reader's feelings about his own speech — public or internal. Suppose that an author wishes to show that one of his creatures is patient or irascible, benign or nervous. If he is skillful he can put into the mouth of that creature language that will touch the experience of the reading community, and thus he can cause the readers to imagine that creature in the intended way. Again, the reader receives clues that revive old impressions; he reassembles these in a new constellation — a new fictional character.

To make these matters explicit renders them obvious. Yet they are of the greatest importance in the novel. They are obvious only because they are so much a part of our experience. But the manner, the precise steps, through which we absorb linguistic facts from the page before us, then out of those facts construct character — that is not obvious at all, and in fact has hardly been touched by scholarship. Perhaps the reason is that the entire matter lies in a no-man's land where criticism, linguistics, psychology and sociology meet. The question is not clearly within the province of any discipline.

It is in this no-man's land that Miss Kaluza[1] is working in the book before us. She has chosen as her material the Benjy, Quentin and Jason sections of *The Sound and the Fury*. She is concerned with the linguistic facts of the monologues, and with the way that the reader uses these facts to construct each of the Compson brothers in imagination. Since the brothers have much of their social identity in common, it is character in the second sense — personality — that concerns our author.

Miss Kaluza has organized her work in five chapters. In the first two she explains her aims and elaborates the type of linguistic analysis to be used. Chapter III is devoted to Benjy's speech, Chapter IV to Quentin's, and Chapter V to Jason's. The first two chapters are crucial to an understanding of the later ones, but are rigorously technical. Moreover, they deal with syntactical theory, which will not be every reader's meat. I shall, therefore, attempt a brief summary of this material in simple language.

The syntactician attempts to answer this question: What sentences exist in English? His answer is a formula of some kind that attempts to imply all the possible English Sentences, but without implying any non-English ones. All sentences, he supposes, are either simple ones or they are some combination of the simple ones. Thus his basic conception is somewhat like the chemist's: there are atoms and there are molecules, but molecules are merely combinations of atoms. The first task in syntax, therefore, is to take inventory of the simple sentences. The next task is to describe how these may be combined to form all the more complex ones.

---

[1] Miss Kaluza bases her work on the English (Chatto and Windus) edition of 1954, and upon the Compson Appendix text published in the 1946 Modern Library edition of *The Sound and the Fury*. The Chatto and Windus was not a happy choice. (For particulars, see James B. Meriwether, "The Textual History of *The Sound and the Fury*," pp. 18-20 in this collection.) Nor does Miss Kaluza always quote it accurately. All quotations from the novel that appear in this review have therefore been corrected according to the original edition (New York: Cape and Smith, 1929). I have also tinkered lightly with some of her citation devices, and have corrected one error in spelling according to her *errata* list.

There are some dozens of types of simple sentences in English. One of them may be described as *subject + linking verb + adjective*, of which an example is *The boy was hungry*. Another simple type is *subject + transitive verb + object*, of which an example is *The boy ate a sandwich*. Each of these types has not just a single exemplification, but millions upon millions, incredible as it may seem. To gain an insight into this matter, it is convenient to imagine a slot machine of the kind that has wheels with pictures of fruit on them. Instead of fruit, imagine that the wheels of the machine have on them subjects, verbs and adjectives that correspond to the parts of our first simple sentence type. When the wheels spin round they stop on combinations that are sentences, as follows:

First Wheel	*Second Wheel*	*Third Wheel*
The boy	was	hungry.
A puppy	seems	young.
The milk	felt	cold.
The paint	smells	fresh.
The beer	tastes	good.
The mixture	turned	purple.
A hypotenuse	looks	straight.
etc.	etc.	etc.

The syntactician (using symbols — not slot machines) prepares such a device for each simple sentence type. Each must somehow include every exemplification of its type, but all non-sentences must be excluded, and here we must make a careful distinction. A sentence like *Them boys is hungry* is English, but it belongs to a sub-standard dialect. The syntactician may allow it or exclude it — depending on what kind of English he is trying to explicate. But *The was hungry boy* is non-English. Innumerable strings of words such as this fail to occur in any dialect, and must be rigorously excluded from our formulas, whatever brand of English we are dealing with. Thus the syntactician is concerned with three kinds of syntax: those sentences that are normal for the dialect that he is treating, those sentences that belong to other dialects, and those strings of words that are not English at all.

But oddly, these three categories do not exhaust the problems that arise in work of this kind, for it happens that most of the sentences implied by our devices fall into none of these categories. To illustrate, the sentences on our wheels above may all seem normal enough, but suppose the wheels spin round and stop on the following combinations:

> A hypotenuse tastes straight.
> The puppy turned fresh.
> The mixture smells hungry.

What are we to make of such utterances? We cannot clearly associate them with any particular social dialect. We cannot exclude them from English altogether, for speakers and writers do make such locutions from time to time. Furthermore, if we try to rule them out, our formulas quickly become so complex as to be unmanageable. We must be content to say that speakers of English have the capacity for making millions upon millions of atoms of each sentence type, but that the great bulk of them are violent metaphors, and are never used. The governing machinery in our brains inhibits our using them, apparently on metaphysical and ontological grounds, for these violent metaphors simply do not describe the world that we know. But these sentences are potential, nevertheless. We shall see later the use to which Faulkner puts this massive fact.

Once having formulated each simple sentence type, the syntactician's next task is to describe how tokens of these types may be combined into larger structures. These descriptions are rather like cooking recipes: one takes ingredients in the form of atomic sentences, reshapes them and combines them to form molecular sentences. Suppose, for example, that we take *The boy was sick* and *The boy was pale* and *The boy was a student*. We can combine the first two with *and*, substituting *he* for one of the subjects. That step yields *The boy was sick and he was pale*. Next we can turn our third atom into a relative clause, insert it precisely after *The boy*, and we get *The boy, who was a student, was sick and he was pale*. Finally, we can apply rules of ellipsis that strike out particular words so as to yield *The boy, a student, was sick and pale*.

In this way the syntactician carefully formulates the manner in which atoms can be combined to form molecular sentences. But at every step he is faced with decisions about the status of the products of his recipes. Some dialects of English make use of some particular rule, but others do not. For example, there are three ways to combine atoms with *because* so as to show a cause-effect relationship between the two. The first of these appears to be the property of every dialect, but the second is more bookish, and the third is downright academic:

1) The boy was pale because he was sick.
2) Because he was sick, the boy was pale.
3) The boy, because he was sick, was pale.

Thus the recipes for forming complex sentences themselves have a dialectal status. Moreover, these recipes never cease to present problems about what is English and what is not. Speakers might, for example, accept all the following as legitimate English sentences:

I could feel water beyond twilight, and could smell it.
I could feel and smell water beyond twilight.
I could feel, smell, water beyond twilight.

But most would say that the following is not English at all:

I could feel water beyond the twilight, smell. [210]

Yet Faulkner made that sentence. It begins to seem doubtful, then, that the theory of syntax can account for empirical sentences, for they are too formidable. The syntactician cannot always make the simple yes-no decisions about them that he would like to make. He therefore turns away from the empirical to deal with idealized, Platonic data — sentences of his own manufacture — in the hope that if the grammar of these can be formulated, the formulas may shed some kind of light upon the more refractory sentences of, say, an Eisenhower press conference, or a Faulkner novel. Thus in one sense we can charge syntactical theory with failure, for it does not clearly account for many of the sentences that people say and write.

But this failure has the very great value that it focuses our attention upon the potentials in language-making. Thus it helps us to understand how the forms of sentences act as an index to the social system, and even give us insight into the mentalities of speakers — in life or in literature. A man or a fictional character speaks, and from the forms of his sentences we the audience, drawing upon our experience and upon the language system stored in our own heads, make deductions about those speakers — make decisions about their social identity, and even about their inner mentality and their outlook upon the world.

It is considerations of these kinds that underlie Miss Kaluza's study of the interior monologues of Benjy, Quentin and Jason.

Benjy's speech is called "The Idiolect of Intuition". (Idiolect means the particular speech of a single person — a dialect of one.) Miss Kaluza sorts the sentences of the Benjy section into three groups. First there are direct quotations, presumably faithful renderings of what the other characters have said in Benjy's presence. The second group are indirect quotations introduced by *he said* and the like. The third group are Benjy's own sentences, about one-fourth of the total. Miss Kaluza calls them "'Benjy's action/perception/thought material". These sentences are marked by a dramatic simplification of the categories of English, a simplification that Faulkner imposes on them with a consistency that suggests the most careful calculation. Since Benjy's sentences are interwoven with the normal quoted material, they are foregrounded — made to stand out — and thus they work their effect on the reader.

Every reader of the Benjy section will have been impressed by the primitive chant-like repetitiveness and the oddness of Benjy's speech. But perhaps few readers will have tried to fix the sources of these effects. Miss Kaluza does just that — with groupings, tables, statistics and some penetrating discussion. She makes explicit the high degree of repetition in Benjy's vocabulary, some of it the repetition of whole sentences — motifs, like "Caddy smelled like trees." She notes Benjy's mechanical associating of name and named: Caddy, for example, is always *Caddy*, never *my sister*, and rarely even *she*. Benjy's lexical resources are scant, and he uses them with a peculiar rigidity.

There is a systematic primitiveness in Benjy's verbs. It happens that English is strikingly rich in the forms of its verbal expressions, which can signal a whole catalogue of aspects in the time relationships among events. But virtually all of Benjy's verbs are in the simple past tense. He uses forms like *took, went* and *smelled;* but forms like *would have taken*, and *was still trying to take* — these are beyond his reach.

Benjy's syntax also is abnormally simple. His sentences are simple atoms, or atoms merely linked with the noncommital *and*:

One Atom:	I couldn't stop. [24]
Two Atoms:	I wasn't crying, and I held to the gate. [64]
Three Atoms:	Then she was crying, and I cried, and we held each other. [58]

Some of these chains grow quite long, but they never lose their simplicity. (Faulkner points up that simplicity by punctuating it with a very simple system: only the period is used terminally, even for questions; only the comma is used internally, and that sparingly.) The frequency of the pale conjunction *and*, which merely makes lists, is an important index to Benjy's mentality, for without recourse to the rich system of English conjunctive machinery, he is unable to show relationships among events. For example, he cannot indicate temporal relations, and so he cannot make such sentences as these:

> Jason read the paper while we played.
> After T. P. had dressed me, we went out.

Likewise, he cannot show cause-and-effect relationships, since he cannot make such sentences as these:

> T. P. took me home, for I was tired.
> Jason cried because Father had whipped him.

Miss Kaluza discusses the function of Benjy's repetition of whole sentences, which has, among other effects, the ironic one of making his speech less monotonous. She also examines his curious metaphorical language, which poses in acute form the syntactician's dilemma about the Englishness to the violent metaphor. In Benjy's universe death can be *smelled*, barns *go away*, and hands *see*.

Thus Benjy's language is strange. In one sense it is primitive — his vocabulary is rigid and poverty-stricken; the normal grammatical categories of time and tense have all been collapsed into one, and so have the conjunctive devices that mark the relations among events. But Benjy's language is rich in one sense, for he can combine subjects and predicates in a way to suggest the familiar world in a strange new way. What Faulkner has done, then, is to recategorize Benjy's language, so that the machinery for signalling the relations among events is nearly abolished, and the categories of subject and object are completely restructured.

This language makes difficult reading, especially since the jumpy flashbacks lack the compositional signals that we expect from narration. Faulkner gives some hints about the time in which things happen for Benjy (the leaves are brown or green; now Luster is the bodyguard, now T. P. or Versh) but these hints never come in the ordinary linguistic way — through the verb system with its satellite adverbs. Benjy has no such expressions.

His world is made up of few things and people, and the relationships among them are a great blur. Miss Kaluza remarks:

> His mind may thus be likened to a moving picture camera, register-
> ing pictures but unable to interpret and arrange them meaning-
> fully. Incidentally, as often happens in Faulkner, the reader must
> take the duties of a montage editor upon himself, if he wants to
> understand the story.

Her conclusions, with a bit of ellipsis, are as follows:

> ... [T]he linguistic structure of Benjy's idiolect ... makes for a very
> peculiar ritualistic stylized language, perfectly systematic in its use
> of linguistic devices and coherent in the ultimate meaning it con-
> veys. ... Benjy's form of apprehension emerges as essentially mono-
> lithic. The only mental operation he is capable of performing is
> that of mechanical identification. Abstractions, distinctions of time,
> space, cause-and-effect, etc., do not exist for him as he has no
> abstracting or logical faculties. Neither is he able to distinguish ...
> objects of external reality, his own body, his sensations, and even his
> own feelings: they all share the same external nature of objects for
> him. In Benjy's oneness of experience there is no realization of
> himself as the focus of his own experience, and finally no realiza-
> tion of the fact of his existence. ...

Quentin's language is called "The Idiolect of Subjectivity".
Here Miss Kaluza's task is far more difficult than in the Benjy
section, for Quentin's mentality is incomparably more complex
than Benjy's, and his language is correspondingly richer and
more varied. Quentin's mental processes range from his detached
narration of small events to the deepest, most perfervid intro-
spection. What Miss Kaluza is at pains to show is that Faulkner
has supplied Quentin with a distinct kind of language to match
each gradation in this range: his narrations of small events are
rendered in the simplest and most transparent language; his
more intense and inward processes are carried out in some of the
most fractured, disordered language that literature can show. Thus
Faulkner uses styles of language to give insight into Quentin's
mental state at a given moment; all the styles taken together
lead the reader to construct the whole of Quentin's complex
personality.

I shall not attempt to recapitulate the elaborate apparatus
through which Miss Kaluza wrings order out of the Quentin

section, but shall merely pick out some of the mental processes that she posits, then give illustrations of the kind of language through which a given process is carried on.

The simplest of Quentin's mental activities is the description of his own actions on the day of his death. He renders these accounts swiftly, and his sentences are merely strings of atomic sentences joined by *and*. Thus his most unimportant mental activities call for speech that is like Benjy's habitual language:

> I put on my new suit and put my watch on and packed the other suit and the accessories and my razor and brushes in my hand bag, and wrapped the trunk key into a sheet of paper and put it in an envelope and addressed it to Father, and wrote the two notes and sealed them. [99-100]

Of such language Miss Kaluza says:

> Quentin's mind is presented as it registers, mechanically and impassively, the trivial chores he is performing with a complete lack of interest.

Next Miss Kaluza posits the mental process that she calls sensory perception. The sentences through which this activity is carried out are marked by a curious structure that is here called the appended group. This device is typically Faulknerian, as every reader will recognize. Here are three examples with the appended groups underlined:

> He was still looking at the watch, *his mouth shaping*. [95]
> The draft in the door smelled of water, *a damp steady breath*. [210-211]
> I could feel water beyond the twilight, *smell*. [210]

What is especially Faulknerian about these appended groups is that, in the syntactician's special sense, they are often ungrammatical. They are not the products of fully English recipes for combining atomic sentences into molecular ones. If a complex sentence is completely grammatical, we can resolve it into its atoms and then state precisely the manner and order in which those atoms may be recombined to produce the complex sentence — much as if we resolved a cake into its original ingredients and then gave the recipe for making that cake. But with many of Faulkner's sentences this is not possible. The atoms are often difficult to determine, and even when determined are themselves often ungrammatical. Nor can one state the processes for their combination with confidence. The following sentence, for example, defies this kind of examination, and incidentally furnishes insight into the syntactician's retreat from empirical sentences to the Platonic ones that can be made to obey his rules:

> The bird whistled again, invisible, a sound meaningless and profound, inflexionless, ceasing as though cut off with the blow of a knife, and again, and that sense of water swift and peaceful above secret places, felt, not seen not heard. [168-169]

We are dealing in this language with those failures of parallelism and those misplaced modifiers that are denied the freshman, but are freely permitted Faulkner, because he has an artistic purpose for them. He enchains the appended groups, sometimes by the dozen; the longer the chain the greater the ambiguity, and the more inward, intense and important the mental process that is attributed to Quentin thereby.

The typical sentence in Quentin's idiom of perception is a complete atom with one or more truncated or deformed ones trailing behind. The finite verb of the main atom often suggests some central action or observation, and the appended groups with their non-finite verbs are satellites to that central point. The result may be something like a "set picture", especially if there is a long trail of appended groups:

> The lane went between back premises — unpainted houses with more of those gay and startling coloured garments on lines, a barn broken-backed, decaying quietly among rank orchard trees, unpruned and weed-choked, pink and white and murmurous with sunlight and with bees. [165]

Sometimes, especially if the sentence abounds in *-ing* forms (that favorite of Faulkner's generally), it conveys intricate and interrelated movements all going on at once:

> The tug came back downstream, the water shearing in long rolling cylinders, rocking the float at last with the echo of passage, the float lurching onto the rolling cylinder with a plopping sound and a long jarring noise as the door rolled back and two men emerged, carrying a shell. [111]

Sometimes the appended groups are experimental in the extreme, and are at their most ambiguous. The reader is left to work out his own interpretation from among several possibilities, or to accept them all:

They saw us from the water first, head and shoulders.

Finally, at the opposite end of the scale from simple narration, we have Quentin's deepest, most turbulent mental processes and the language that signifies them. That language is here called the idiom of memory and reflection. It is the most fractured of all. A sample will suffice to remind the reader what it is like:

> ... *getting the odour of honeysuckle all mixed She would have told me not to let me sit there on the steps hearing her door twilight slamming hearing Benjy still crying Supper she would have to come down then getting honeysuckle all mixed up in it.* ... [160]

Miss Kaluza goes on to make many observations about these styles and their functions, and in arguments too long to be given succinctly, she shows rather convincingly that there is rhetorical organization in some of this material. It involves, for example, complex parallelisms. Miss Kaluza points out that these devices sometimes resscue Quentin's language from total obscurity, since it is without the usual kinds of order.

In the summary of her findings and impressions, Miss Kaluza says of Quentin's language:

> It explores various levels of consciousness, from the more or less coherent registration of action and sensory perception, through the confusion and emotional intensity of memory, to the vision-like clarity of the subconscious. Through it Quentin's mind gets characterized as complex, quick, intelligent and sensitive, but emotionally unstable and prone to obsession.

She then emphasizes the resemblance of Quentin's language to Faulkner's own — to Faulkner's more subjective language generally and specifically to the language of the omniscient author of the fourth section of *The Sound and the Fury*. She thinks this resemblance important:

> Critics have often argued that in the Faulkner-Quentin relation there is a lack of the distance that Faulkner usually observes towards his characters. The linquistic facts presented in this chapter verify this impressionistic judgment.

Jason's language, with a hint of irony, is called "The Idiolect of Rationalism". His speech differs from Quentin's in that it does not seem to well from the depths of Jason's psyche. Perhaps that effect was calculated to suggest that Jason's mentality has no great depth. Miss Kaluza credits the Faulkner scholars with saying that this is no longer internal monologue, and credits one with calling it "soliloquy on a surface, communicating level." Jason even holds conversation with himself:

> The time before I says that's the last one now; you'll have to remember to get some more right away. [268]

Jason's speech is larded with sub-standard grammar and idiom. A few examples will give the flavor:

> he was bad fooled [262]
> There's a man right here in Jefferson made a lot of money [241]
> I hadn't got out of sight of his barn hardly [299]
> He made like he was busy

Such expressions stand out, but generally Jason's language is characterized by that looseness of construction and pervasive disorder that the composition teacher is reduced to calling *awk*, for in its imprecision it cannot even be precisely defined. Miss Kaluza does, however, manage some generalizations.

Where Benjy uses *and* in such a way that no relationship at all is shown among his clauses, and where Quentin uses *and* to enchain small events in what we take to be strict temporal sequence, Jason uses *and* to join clauses of unequal rank. These sentences are hard to describe, but they have their effect on the reader nevertheless. Here is Jason on two occasions in the manner of the folkwife reciting some burning injustice:

> After all the risk I'd taken . . . and me having to tell Mother lies about it. [262]

> I'd have to drop everything and run to sell some redneck a dime's worth of nails or something, and Earl up there gobbling a sandwich. . . . [263]

Other connectives, like *because*, Jason uses so often and so loosely that they become as pale and functionless as his *and's*:

> So he kept on patting her hand . . . with one of the black gloves that we got the bill for four days later because it was the twenty-sixth because it was the same day one month that Father went up there and got it and brought it home . . . and I says,

"Well, they brought my job home tonight" because all the time we
kept hoping they'd get things straightened out and he'd keep her
because Mother kept saying she would at least have enough regard
for the family not to jeopardize my chance after she and Quentin
had had theirs. [245-246]

Jason uses pronouns without much regard for a hearer's con-
venience:

. . . how can they expect anybody to control her, with her giving her
money behind our backs. [262]

Also, the antecedantless *they* is everywhere in Jason's speech.
The conjectures in brackets are Miss Kaluza's:

He's going to keep on running up and down that fence and bellowing every time they [golfers?] come in sight until first thing I
know they're [golf course authorities?] going to begin charging me
golf dues. . . . Then they'd [town authorities?] send us all to Jackson, maybe. God knows, they'd [patients in the Jackson asylum?]
hold Old Home week when that happened. [232]

Miss Kaluza makes more generalizations of this sort, and while
her conclusions seem valid as far as they go, she simply cannot
muster very much to say about Jason beyond the obvious. She
has used twenty pages to treat Benjy, and thirty for Quentin,
but Jason gets a scant ten. It is the least cogent chapter of
her book.

Jason is hard to analyze, not because he is unclear, but because we cannot look at him sympathetically or even objectively.
For one thing, he is not *simpatico*. Faulkner has laden him with
every form of moral leprosy. He hates niggers and Jews and
foreigners. He cheats. Unlike Benjy, who cannot distinguish his
ego from the rest of the cosmos, Jason sees everything as either
Jason or non-Jason. And the non-Jason is conspiratorial. He is
vulgar and belligerently unapologetic. The reader apprehends him
with the greatest clarity, but because he is repellent he is difficult
to analyze with the same care that produced him.

For another thing, Jason's language is hard to analyze because
it is so ordinary. Jason is constructed out of folk English. Where
Benjy's speech and Quentin's are foregrounded against the background of the everyday and the ordinary, Jason's speech *is* the
everyday and ordinary, and that is hard to describe.

And it is hard to produce. I wish to emphasize the mastery that Faulkner demonstrates in the language that he gives Jason to say. Time after time it rings utterly true to the speech of northern Mississippi, and to a personality type that we have all met. To some degree the depicting of Benjy and Quentin is purely intellectual: we have no direct experience with the internal language of an idiot, and none with the elegant distortions of Quentin's language except as to some degree it resembles that of our own internal musings. But with Jason's language Faulkner reflects a part of the world that at least some of us have known. To have sustained this monologue in folk English, speaking thereby so directly to the reader's experience, strikes this reviewer as a greater triumph than the creation of either Benjy or Quentin, both of whom we must accept in something of an intellectual spirit.

There is more to say about Jason's speech. Since Jason himself is repellent, I think we tend to dismiss the occasional power with which he speaks. There is sometimes a direct quality about it — like machine gun fire. But since Jason is unadmirable, and since folk English in such a person loses its charming harmlessness and grows socially potent and thus itself unadmirable, we cannot bring ourselves to admire Jason's speech, even when it has considerable force.

There is one final point. Miss Kaluza does not sufficiently emphasize that it is entirely in their inner personalities that Benjy and Quentin are depicted, while Jason not only is given his personality but is also supplied a social identity that we do not expect. For this is not the language of Compsons, but the language of the folk. I leave it to the critics to decide what Faulkner is telling us with that fact. But it must be of some importance. It is not usual for the son to slide down from the language of Father Compson to the language of Jason. Whatever the meaning, Jason's language seems to this reviewer to be art of a high order. It is just that we are not psychologically prepared to examine it with the great care that it merits.

Miss Kaluza sums up Jason with a comparison:

> In fact all the linguistic features of Jason's idiolect, including the vocabulary which has not been examined here, contribute to make it a common speech medium. . . . It is devastatingly characteristic of Jason that he never allows his mental experience to operate beyond the conscious speech level, and always tries, by indefatigably inserting words like *because, when, where* and *if,* to organize his experi-

ence logically. But the result is far from logical, and his efforts are futile. Thus he always aspires to rationality without ever achieving it in fact.

There follows a "Conclusion" in which Miss Kaluza summarizes what she thinks she has learned and shown. I quote the following bit, which seems central:

> Now these three contrastive syntactic systems underlie the structure of *The Sound and the Fury* not only by differentiating characters, their mental and emotional make-up, their levels of consciousness (Benjy's and Jason's operating on one level only, while Quentin's is multilevelled) and the mood and tempo of the flow of their mental content, but also by providing through these characters three different perspectives from which to view and interpret the events and the novel's ultimate meaning: the intuitive perspective of Benjy, the emotional-subjective of Quentin, and the pseudo-rational of Jason. In effect *The Sound and the Fury* is one of those rare works where the subject and form are inextricably blended, the one illumining the other.

A footnote appended to the above also seems worth quoting:

> Where no such happy unity exists, the hazards of Faulkner's method become very obvious. In *A Fable* for instance many syntactic structures are similar to those in *The Sound and the Fury*, but, since no unity is achieved between the allegorical subject and Faulkner's "concrete" language, they are reduced to the status of mere devices with no function to perform (they could hardly be called ornamental). As a result the style fashioned by these structures is artificial and often pretentious.

Or to put this thought in the language with which this review began — when Faulkner's style has no function to perform, but merely is the author's presence, it can be indigestible and annoying.

Miss Kaluza's book ends on this note. The bibliography gives a few final insights into her preparation. She has evidently read a lot of Faulkner criticism and many linguistic works. These latter give some understanding of her rather eclectic linguistic philosophy, which is taken from all manner of schools and persuasions.

Miss Kaluza's book is hard to read, not because she is a poor writer, for she is a rather good one, especially considering that English seems not be her native tongue. The book is hard because

it is hard. We have not much experience in reading about literature as it is attacked in this way. Furthermore, the book is directed
to no particular audience. The more ideological linguists will ignore
it because of its doctrinal eclecticism and because it has to do
with literature; and the book will not be the rage among critics,
for it will take much determination for the non-linguist to plow
through the technical notions and apparatus. Moreover, the book
is surprisingly marred with misspellings and small errors, only a
fraction of which are accounted for in the *errata* sheet that is
taped inside the front cover.

Yet I think this book has considerable value. It is an attempt
to trace a connection between the linguistic facts of a novel and
the states of response that the work induces in the reader. Some
critics may be content to celebrate those states; some linguists
may be content merely to catalogue the facts. And in any event
it is a formidable matter to look for the connection between the
two. But language is the raw material of literature; therefore, the
language of a novel cannot be irrelevant to the value of that
novel, and some scholars will keep trying to find the connection,
which leads through the deepest parts of ourselves — through our
unanalyzed cognition of the world as it is presented in language.
Miss Kaluza's book is an attempt to find a path from fact to
state. Her attempt is tentative, to be sure. But someday perhaps
through such efforts, the language scholar and the critic will catch
a glimpse of each other through the foliage, and will realize with
a start that they really have been laboring in the same vineyard
all the time.